About the Editors

Patricia A. O'Hare, Dr.P.H., M.S., R.N., is Assistant Professor of Nursing at Georgetown University School of Nursing, and Clinical Research Director for a Health Care Financing Administration (HCFA) funded project on home care. She is currently a curriculum advisory board member of the National Institute for Discharge Planning and Continuity of Care, and a consultant in discharge planning/ continuing care. She is chairing a national committee of the American Association for Continuity of Care to explore the issue of certification for continuing care professionals. Dr. O'Hare has conducted research on the discharge planning process.

Margaret A. Terry, M.S., A.N.P.C., R.N., is on the faculty of the Graduate Program in Home Health Administration at the School of Nursing, The Catholic University of America. She is a consultant to home health agencies, hospitals, and geriatric facilities, and prior to her faculty position, was Associate Director for Community and Home Health Services at the Greater Southeast Community Hospital in Washington, D.C., where she developed a hospital-wide discharge planning program involving multiple disciplines. Ms. Terry planned, organized, and managed a hospital-based home health agency and a freestanding home health agency. She is a board member and now secretary of Capital Home Health Association in Washington, D.C. Ms. Terry has spoken at national conferences on home health and geriatric issues.

DISCHARGE PLANNING

STRATEGIES FOR FOR ASSURING CONTINUITY OF CARE

Contributors

Karen Arcidiacono, R.Ph., J.D.
Associate Counsel
Greater Southeast Community
Hospital
Washington, D.C.

Susan Coleman, M.P.H., R.N.
Executive Director
Hunt Country Home Health
Reston, Virginia

Elaine M. Frank, M.H.S.
Director, Program and Human
Development
Greater Southeast Center for the
Aging
Washington, D.C.

Charlotte A. Leavitt, B.S.N., R.N.
Director, Continuing Care
Department
Framingham Union Hospital
Framingham, Massachusetts

**Sally Anne McCarthy, M.S.N.,
P.N.P., R.N.**
Continuity of Care/Discharge
Planning Specialist
Children's Hospital National
Medical Center
Washington, D.C.

**Michael P. O'Brien, M.S.W.,
C.S.W., A.C.S.W.**
Executive Director
Patient Assistance Foundation
Pacific Presbyterian Medical
Center
San Francisco, California

Kay L. Rogers, M.P.H., R.N.
Manager of Continuing Care
Department
Group Health, Inc.
Minneapolis, Minnesota

**Lester W. Scheuermann, M.S.W.,
A.C.S.W., L.C.S.W.**
Coordinator, Geriatric Services
Greater Southeast Community
Hospital
Washington, D.C.

DISCHARGE PLANNING

STRATEGIES FOR ASSURING CONTINUITY OF CARE

Edited by

Patricia A. O'Hare, Dr.P.H., M.S., R.N.
Assistant Professor of Nursing
Georgetown University School of Nursing
Washington, D.C.

Margaret A. Terry, M.S., A.N.P.C., R.N.
Faculty
Graduate Program in Home Health Administration
Catholic University School of Nursing
Washington, D.C.

AN ASPEN PUBLICATION®
Aspen Publishers, Inc.

1988

Rockville, Maryland
Royal Tunbridge Wells

Library of Congress Cataloging-in-Publication Data

Discharge planning : strategies for assuring continuity of care /
[edited by] Patricia A. O'Hare, Margaret S. Terry.
p. cm.
"An Aspen publication."
Includes bibliography and index.
ISBN 0-87189-895-0
1. Health facilities—Discharge planning. 2. Continuum of care.
I. O'Hare, Patricia A. II. Terry, Margaret A.
[DNLM: 1. Patient Care Planning. 2. Patient Discharge. 3. After
Care. WX 158 D611]
RA971.8.D573 1988
362.1'1—dc19
DNLM/DLC
for Library of Congress
87-30643
CIP

This publication is intended to provide accurate and authorative information in regard
to the Subject Matter covered. It is sold with the understanding that the publisher is
not engaged in rendering legal, accounting, or other professional service. If legal advice
or other expert assistance is required, the service of a competent professional person
should be sought. (From a *Declaration of Principles* jointly adopted by a committee of
the American Bar Association and a committee of Publishers and Associations.)

Editorial Services: Carolyn Ormes

Library of Congress Catalog Card Number: 87-30643
ISBN: 0-87189-895-0

Printed in the United States of America

1   2   3   4   5

To my husband Bill,
and children Kevin and Sheila

P.O'H.

To my family: Willie, Christopher, and Douglas

M.A.T.

Contents

Foreword

As those who follow or are providers of health care know first-hand, our current health care system is undergoing what may prove to be the most significant economic and social transformation since the enactment of Medicare and Medicaid. The move to prospective reimbursment in diagnosis-related groups (DRGs) for hospitals under Medicare, the effects of the growing federal budget deficit on reimbursement levels for all providers under Medicare and Medicaid, and growing pressures for cost containment in both the public and private sections have greatly influenced the profile of our service system and have raised concerns about health care quality and access. At the same time, debate over the need for catastrophic health care coverage has heightened our awareness of the needs of uninsured Americans and of those who are underinsured against the costs of long-term care.

In this context, and in response to the potential negative effects of cost containment on beneficiary access to hospital and post-hospital care, the roles of case management and discharge planning have gained importance. These functions will continue to be viewed as cornerstones of quality and efficient health care throughout the debate over catastrophic health care and long-term care financing.

As a former social worker, I fully appreciate the central role that case management plays for individuals and for the health care svstem as a whole. Discharge planners work with the patients, their families, and community providers to coordinate the resources that best accommodate the patients' medical, social, economic, and emotional needs and to ensure smooth transitions between levels of care. Discharge planners go further and promote effective and efficient coordination of services, preventing fragmentation in our rapidly changing health care system.

This timely book presents facts and offers suggestions regarding discharge planning and the concepts of continuing care and case management. These can be utilized to decrease costs without sacrificing health care quality or access. As such, I commend the achievements and efforts of the authors. Dr. Patricia O'Hare has demonstrated her commitment and expertise in the health care field in her work as a clinical nurse specialist in community health, through her doctoral research in discharge planning, and as Assistant Professor on the faculty of the Georgetown University School of Nursing. Ms. Margaret Terry has exhibited her expertise in health care, and in discharge planning specifically, as a public health nurse, in her design of a continuing care program and hospital-based home care program, and in her current position on the faculty of the home health administration at The Catholic University of America in Washington, D.C.

As Chairman of the House Select Committee on Aging, I remain committed to the goal of a comprehensive and coordinated system of health and long-term care services for all Americans. As we move forward toward this goal, I know that health care providers such as the readers of this volume will continue to enhance their knowledge and skills. I'm confident that these providers will be well prepared to meet the new demands for coordinated, high quality, efficient, and effective care by the time the Congress finds the will to put such a system into place.

Edward R. Roybal, Chairman
House Select Committee on Aging

Preface

The purpose of this book is to discuss the essentials of discharge planning and its importance in the current health care environment. The current environmental and regulatory issues that affect discharge planning will be presented, highlighting the new urgency for health care administrators and discharge planners to establish effective discharge planning programs.

The survival of hospitals, long-term care facilities, home health agencies, and health maintenance organizations depends on providing the most appropriate level of care in the most efficient and timely manner. The book discusses the increasing importance of the discharge planning process as health care agencies and facilities attempt to meet this ever-changing challenge. It also provides the framework for administrators and health care providers to establish, manage, and evaluate a discharge planning program. The strategies for development of practice models for discharge planning in a multitude of health care settings are reviewed.

The discharge planner will be armed with the communication and management skills needed to operate in a role where power and authority must be earned, not just assumed. The planner will also receive a thorough description of federal regulations and reimbursement changes, accrediting body standards, and association standards. Attention is directed to linkages with community resources to effectively plan and coordinate services. We will discuss and confront the professional and ethical dilemmas faced by health care providers as they attempt to facilitate continuity of care as demands and constraints increase and resources decrease.

The book includes a discussion of the future of discharge planning in an aging society, where cost containment is a public policy mandate. We then explore the incentives for the development of the discharge planning function. Finally, we stress the necessity of developing linkages in a limited-resource, cost-efficient environment.

Acknowledgments

Our thanks to those who commented on the manuscript or who helped in other ways with the book—our husbands Bill and Willie, Ty Cullen, and Nancy Smith.

A special thanks to our contributors, who stated so clearly the issues in continuing care from their perspectives and in their respective settings.

We also appreciate the cooperation and assistance provided by Darlene Como and the Aspen editorial staff, especially Carolyn Ormes.

Part I

Introduction

Chapter 1

An Overview of Discharge Planning

Patricia A. O'Hare

1

Discharge planning is assessing needs and obtaining or coordinating appropriate resources for patients and clients as they move through the health care system. The term discharge planning suggests a process that occurs when a person is discharged from a facility or an agency. It is more appropriately termed continuity of care planning.

As one of the major elements in the overall delivery of health care today, discharge planning is the interorganizational link for establishing or operationalizing the system of continuing care. It is practiced by many with varying degrees of sophistication and knowledge. Patients, families, and professionals attempt to provide the linkage and cement in the non-system of health care.

The process of discharge planning has been most fully developed in the hospital. There its importance is even more critical today, with the advent of the prospective payment system (PPS) and the resulting need to move patients quickly from acute to other levels of care. The need to implement and strengthen continuity of care planning outside of hospitals is seen as even more significant as fewer patients enter hospitals and community-based services become the primary mode of health care delivery.

The environmental and regulatory issues that have created a new urgency for effective discharge planning will be examined. Health care practice and delivery are shaped by a complex of financial incentives, mandatory regulations, consumer needs, and technological advances. The current environment demands the establishment of effective discharge planning programs in all sectors of the health care system.

This chapter looks to the early development of discharge planning functions to shed light on their current status and acceptance. This brief historical perspective will promote understanding of the past and the present and help continuing care professionals to better anticipate future trends.

DISCHARGE PLANNING—A HISTORICAL PERSPECTIVE

Discharge planning is not a new concept. Some referral systems for continuity of nursing care started as early as 1910.[1] At Bellevue Hospital in New York City their publication *Charities and the Commons* (1906–07) refers to "a nurse whose entire time and care is given to befriending those about to be discharged. She inquires into their circumstances, finds out whether they have home or friends to return to; if necessary, secures admission for them into some other curative or consolatory refuge."[2] This service at Bellevue was modeled after a program developed the previous year at Massachusetts General Hospital by Dr. Richard C. Cabot, which used the services of a social worker in the dispensary to get additional information about the patient. This additional information was then used as a "means for more accurate diagnosis and more effective treatment."[3] These two examples are indeed significant because they were the beginnings of a continuing care model of service. Yet we have not seen this process flourish because of the predominant medical model and the previous financial incentives for hospital-based care rather than care in the community. There is currently renewed interest in discharge planning because of PPS in the hospital sector.

In one early study (1962) Smith[4] identified the need for discharge planning and suggested the specific concepts of patient teaching and follow-up services, especially home care, for patients discharged from hospitals. Another publication, Edith Wensley's *Nursing Service Without Walls*, urged hospitals to emphasize planning for home care services and stated criteria that were useful in alerting hospital staff to patient needs for referral to community services. The criteria suggested by the findings of Smith's study are worth noting. The criteria to alert hospital staff to patient needs for referral to community services were as follows:

- The complexity of a procedure, as administration of a medicine or a treatment, that requires professional assistance in the home.
- An indication that a patient and/or family are unable to give care or do not understand directions for follow-up care.
- Signs that the patient and/or family are unable to accept or are disturbed by some aspect of the condition or care.
- Evidence of need for reinforcement and clarification of instruction started in the hospital.
- The expressed needs of patients for follow-up nursing ser-

vice when professional personnel have corroborated the appropriateness of public health nursing to meet the needs.

- Some aspect of the physical or social environment at home and outside the hospital that may interfere with a patient's satisfactory self-care, for instance, an elderly patient living alone or with an elderly spouse, or at a distance from the hospital that makes frequent trips to the clinic difficult.[5]

In August 1966 the Steering Committee of the National League for Nursing (NLN) Division of Nursing Services, composed of members of the steering committees of the Department of Hospital Nursing and the Department of Public Health Nursing, strongly recommended that

every hospital, every nursing home, every home nursing care agency, if it has not already done so, take the following steps:

1. Appoint some one person, preferably on a full-time basis, to work with staff members in developing plans for the next stage of nursing care, even as the present stage is being provided.
2. Develop well-defined, clearly written procedures for patient referral, and interpret them to the entire staff.
3. Confer on the appointed person the administrative authority to carry out the continuity program.
4. Delegate to the appointed person responsibility for effective planning and on-going communication with appropriate service agencies.[6]

Medicare and Medicaid play a strong role in health care financing and health care delivery. Medicare (Title XVIII) and Medicaid (Title XIX) were 1965 amendments to the Social Security Act, implemented July 1, 1966. Yet 20 years after the passage of this legislation and the statement of the NLN on continuity of care there were, and possibly still are, hospitals in the United States where discharge planning was just beginning to be instituted as an essential component of comprehensive quality care.[7] Discharge planning can no longer be considered a nicety; it has become a necessity. Effective as of September 15, 1986, the new Conditions of Participation for Hospitals for the Medicare and Medicaid Programs include the standard for discharge planning under quality assurance. This regulation requires the hospital to have "an effective, ongoing discharge planning program that facilitates the provision of follow-up care."[8] Discharge planning has moved from a service that, if it existed at all, was primarily carried out by a single provider, either a nurse or a social worker, to a program implemented by multiple providers as part of a multidisciplinary team.[9–15]

DIRECTIONAL FORCES THAT INFLUENCE CONTINUITY OF CARE

Historically, legislation such as Medicare and Medicaid, and the establishment of Professional Standards Review Organizations (PSROs) have affected hospital discharge planning. The implementation of Medicare required the establishment of a utilization review committee in every hospital to review the appropriateness of services and the lengths of stay. Further emphasis on discharge planning came in 1972, when amendments to the Social Security Act created PSROs to monitor the necessity and cost of medical care. These review mechanisms provided the real impetus for the growth and emphasis on discharge planning in hospitals.[16,17] This development has been further reinforced by the standards of the Joint Commission on Accreditation of Hospitals (JCAH).

The Social Security Act amendments of 1983 provided sweeping changes in the area of hospital reimbursement for Medicare patients. Title VI of Public Law 98-21[18] provided that hospitals would receive payment prospectively for services to Medicare patients on the basis of 467 diagnosis-related groups (DRGs). This legislation provided a major impetus for hospitals to further reduce their lengths of stay, and thus had major implications for the growing field of discharge planning. As a result of the legislation it became a priority, and in fact a financial necessity, for each Medicare patient to attain the shortest length of stay possible, which increased the caseloads of discharge planners.[19] It became apparent that with community caseloads increasing as a result of earlier hospital discharges, realistic discharge planning was needed in all sectors of the health care delivery system.

Legislative Controls and Reimbursement Issues

The DRG-based reimbursement program, called the prospective payment system (PPS), provides incentives for hospitals to hold down costs. PPS for Medicare patients gives acute care hospitals a financial incentive to send patients home sooner. The prospective rate is based on each patient's diagnosis and is paid per hospital stay, regardless of actual costs incurred. Before PPS, hospitals were reimbursed for Medicare services on a cost-for-service-provided basis. This was done retrospectively and carried no incentive for cost control, since the more a hospital expended, the more Medicare paid.

The PPS began to be phased in on October 1, 1983. Under Medicare's PPS, during the first year only 25 percent of the reimbursement was based on the assigned DRG, with the remaining 75 percent based on what the specific hospital would have charged under the retrospective system. In the second year the national figure totaled 50 percent, in the third year 75 percent, and after that time 100 percent. This gradual fiscal tightening has given the hospitals some time to look at their systems and make adjustments.

The principal diagnosis—the one that is the major cause of the hospital admission—determines the DRG length of stay, and thus the level of payment. Age, complications, and comorbidities are taken into consideration. An understanding of PPS is necessary to fully appreciate the increasing necessity of discharge planning in health care today and in the future.

The PPS and its effects cannot be separated from the effects of Peer Review Organizations (PROs). The two are intertwined and will each exert major changes on the use of hospital services and the overall delivery of health care. The PROs replaced the PSROs, which were generally viewed as ineffective in controlling costs. Implementation of the PROs began in October 1984.

According to its contract with the Health Care Financing Administration (HCFA), a PRO is required to review services provided by physicians, other health care practitioners, and suppliers. Its responsibilities include review of health care services funded under Medicare to determine whether or not those services are reasonable, are medically necessary, are furnished at the appropriate level of care, and meet professional standards. Contracts between HCFA and PROs are for two years and are renewable.[20] Each PRO negotiates with the Department of Health and Human Services (DHHS) regarding the individual criteria to be used in its reviews, and the PRO then identifies the diagnoses, conditions, procedures, and so on for focused review.[21] The contracts must specify objectives to be achieved during the contract period. The PRO will be evaluated on the basis of the achievement of these objectives. The focus of the PROs is broader than that of the PSROs, and the evaluation component is an integral part of the program. In an attempt to eliminate possible premature discharges, HCFA insists that the PROs do intensified reviews, which entails assessing the adequacy of discharge planning and a documented plan for appropriate follow-up care when such plans are indicated.[22]

In some instances the PRO may determine that care could have been provided at a different level but that such resources were not available in the community. This has major implications for discharge planners, whose roles and responsibilities are expanding to include making the community aware of the need for certain resources and then working toward developing such resources. There is a need to address both quality of care and access to post-hospital care. Data need to be gathered regarding the level or type of care people are receiving post discharge, who is providing the care, and the cost of that care.

For discharge planners, who are also functioning as patient advocates, sometimes the relationship with the PRO will be adversarial because the planners will be dissatisfied with determinations made by the PRO. These encounters, however, have the potential for providing a more realistic picture of health care services and of the need for eventually broadening and strengthening these services. This implies that discharge planners must be not only clinically competent, but also politically astute. It also implies that research studies need to be designed and carried out to measure the effectiveness of discharge planning, especially in terms of such outcomes as patient health status, patient satisfaction, and appropriateness of postdischarge services.

PROs are currently looking only at hospital care, but this situation is likely to expand to include reviewing services in nursing homes, home health agencies, health maintenance organizations (HMOs), physicians' offices, and so forth. Continuity of care planning from all of these areas is needed. Nursing homes are no longer terminal placements, but are increasingly becoming part of the continuum of care. Home health agencies can no longer afford to carry clients indefinitely. HMOs, in practicing preventive medicine and decreasing the number of hospitalizations, must consider how the person is managing, or will manage, his or her own care and if and when in-home services are needed. Physicians in private practice must also be involved in continuity of care planning with their patients. The following case study will illustrate.

Case Study

A 70-year-old man with diagnoses of hypertension, diabetes, and congestive heart failure, who has ascites, leg edema, and leg ulcers, was hospitalized within the past six months for an in-depth medical evaluation. When his condition recently worsened, his physician told him that there was no reason for him to be hospitalized this time. Instead, he was told to go home, increase his medication, rest, elevate his feet, change the dressing on his leg ulcers, and take care of himself. If, however, the physician had included continuity of care planning in his practice, consideration would be given to how this man was going to manage. What does he understand about his condition? Are he and his wife able to manage the care? What about services in the community, such as a community health nurse to assess the home situation, to continue teaching him and his family, to provide support and health counseling, and to supervise and monitor the care? The social worker from the home health agency, in collaboration with the nurse and the physician, would do a psychosocial assessment, assist with concerns regarding cost of services, identify other community resources, and provide emotional support to the client and the family as needed. In the absence of such an approach, services of a home health agency were not even discussed with the patient and his wife. The services may eventually be obtained but only because the family may learn through friends, neighbors, or another provider that they can call in a referral themselves to request services. Obtaining the orders from the physician and having the in-depth communication that is necessary to provide comprehensive coordinated care may be problems at that time.

There are countless other examples that are more complex, where a multitude of services, such as rehabilitation therapy, homemaker, personal care aide, Meals-on-Wheels, and Lifeline, might be needed in the home. For the person who does not enter the hospital, the physician's office will need to offer continuity of care planning. For some, this will be a new focus. For others, it may have been carried out on a limited basis in the past, but now it must be done in a systematic fashion as an integral part of the care provided in the physician's office. Such planning has numerous implications for both the providers and the recipients of care.

Role of the Client, Family, and Significant Other in Health Care

People who are ill, and their families, need to be seen as active participants in health care and in the continuity of care process. People who are hospitalized have a right not only to be informed of the medical diagnosis(es) and treatment(s), but also to be actively involved in decision making regarding their plan of care both in the hospital and post hospitalization. It means being aware of what the term level of care means so as to understand alternative delivery sites and when their use is appropriate. It means being told what resources are available in the community and what services these resources actually provide. It means knowing what their insurance will and will not pay for and under what conditions.

It means becoming involved in their own self-care, knowing what to do and why. If self-care is not possible, it means that a family member or significant other must learn about the care that is required and provide it with assistance, if necessary, from community agencies. Patients and families, as active participants in care, may not agree with the plan of care suggested by the professionals; for example, the wife who decides to take her husband home rather than place him in a nursing home, although it was questionable whether one person could provide the care needed, even with intermittent skilled nursing visits from a community nursing agency. In such a case a backup plan is needed. The caring and support of the discharge planning team can affect the outcome for both patient and wife.

Additional support and planning by the community provider continue to assist the patient and his wife in attaining services as the needs and situation change. These community linkages are essential in achieving the continuum of care.

For the person being treated outside the hospital, the role of active participant is also vital. The consumer of health care needs to become aware of the realities of health care delivery and community resources. Providers need to assume an active role in this education process.

Ethical and Legal Considerations

When patients' rights of self-determination and access to health care seem compromised, ethical dilemmas may occur. In this time of prospective payment and decreasing lengths of stay, hospital policies to quickly discharge patients may impinge on the rights of patients, creating an ethical dilemma for discharge planners. Further, as hospitals diversify and joint ventures become more common, discharge planners may find themselves being pressured to place patients in certain facilities or to refer only to certain home health agencies without consideration of which agency can best meet the patient's needs. The matching of the patient's needs and the community resource(s) is an essential consideration. Vertical integration of hospital services cannot be allowed to become the only consideration for referrals.

This also raises the question of whether or not the current community health care system is able to meet the needs of discharged patients. Patients are being discharged sooner and sicker than ever before.[23] This increases the need for high-technology care in the community. Are existing community resources sufficient to provide a highly skilled level of care? Are patients and family members being adequately prepared to provide the care? In addition, are the resources available in sufficient numbers in the community to offer the supportive services, such as homemakers, personal care aides, adult day-care centers, transportation, and others, that are needed? Finally, are they affordable and accessible to those who need them? Reimbursement is primarily for medically related services, and funding for social support services is being decreased or eliminated. These social support services are important considerations because of the older, more frail, sicker population in the community who have ongoing needs.

Who will be held accountable for the services and supplies provided by community agencies and medical equipment companies? How will these areas be monitored? With joint ventures, contractual relationships, and the multicorporate systems, who really has the responsibility for monitoring these concerns? Does the consumer know who to turn to?

Legal issues associated with discharge planning, including the areas of professional liability, such as informed consent, antitrust, and Medicare fraud and abuse, will be covered. Ways to reduce the discharge planner's and the hospital's risk of liability will be explored. This includes the discharge planner's understanding of inappropriate referrals and placements. Reasonable care must be taken when making or receiving a referral. The discharge planner cannot be held liable unless he or she knows, or should have known, that the agency or nursing home could not handle the referral.

Documentation, as essential not only to communication and coordination, but also to a legal defense, will also be discussed. The documentation of patient and family teaching, using behavioral terms, indicates the patient's and family's level of learning. For example, the nurse would record that the patient listed the signs and symptoms of hypoglycemia, or that the patient demonstrated how to draw up the correct dose of insulin in the insulin syringe. The role of policies, procedures, and standards will be emphasized.

The patient's and family's perception of the hospital stay is all important. Lawsuits are more likely to be initiated when the patient feels that he or she was not treated like a person who was hurting, or that he or she was ignored. Patient satisfaction, even though subjective, is important. Ethical and legal issues are discussed in greater depth in Chapter 6.

Standards of Practice

The Joint Commission on Accreditation of Hospitals (JCAH) has formulated standards that affect discharge planning. In the *1987 Accredita-*

tion Manual for Hospitals the section on social work services clearly states that "to facilitate continuity of care, assistance is provided to the patient and the patient's family in adapting to the patient care plan, whether the service provided is to be continued in a home care or out-of-home care setting."[24] The section on nursing services indicates that, using the nursing process, a plan of care is documented, reflecting current standards of nursing practice, and that "as appropriate, such measures should include physiological, psychosocial, and environmental factors; patient/family education; and patient discharge planning."[25] In addition, each discipline involved in discharge planning has its own professional standards of practice.

Standards may be hospital specific or region specific. Discharge planning standards of practice were recently developed by a committee of the American Association for Continuity of Care (AACC) to provide safeguards for both patients and providers. They were voted on and approved by the general membership of AACC in December 1986. A copy of the AACC Standards for Hospital Continuity of Care and Code of Ethics are included in Chapter 5. Now that the Standards have been approved they will be sent to JCAH with a strong urging that they be adopted. In addition, AACC is discussing certification for continuing care professionals. Certification would also assure the consumer of a predetermined level of expertise.

Interagency and Interprofessional Competition

Competition is a reality in health care today as organizations vie for the shrinking health care dollar. It is the result of several factors. There has been a proliferation of new agencies, especially proprietary home health agencies, to provide needed services in the community. More and more hospitals are establishing their own home care programs, acquiring durable medical equipment companies, and entering into joint ventures with established certified home health agencies. Where will all of this lead? Which agencies will survive? Will it be those that provide quality services? Is competition creating a market in which cost is more important than quality and service? How will these changes affect health care delivery?

Interprofessional competition, or the turf issue, also needs to be addressed. Although competition is usually healthy, competition between the two main disciplines involved in discharge planning, nursing and social work, can be detrimental to the professionals, to the patients, and to health care delivery. This issue was addressed most creatively by a preconference task force consisting of nurses, social workers, and one physician at a national conference on continuity of care sponsored by AACC. It will be explored under the new team approach and professional turf issues in Chapter 3. Of primary importance is that the interprofessional competition be acknowledged and that effective strategies for working within the situation be developed.

WHY DO DISCHARGE PLANNING?

From an administrator's point of view, effective discharge planning is essential to the financial viability and survival of the organization. It allows the hospital to reasonably decrease the length of hospitalization and yet avoid being accused of forcing "premature discharges." Through effective discharge planning the hospital is able to assure patients and families that every needed and available service has been secured for their care. In today's competitive health care environment discharge planning can represent a strong public relations tool to market the hospital to the community as a caring organization. An effective discharge planning program provides the mechanism for targeting groups of patients with specific needs who can be cared for in alternative settings. For example, identifying patients who have been hospitalized for intravenous antibiotic therapy that can now be provided at home through the hospital-based home care program or a community-based home health agency can both reduce costs and improve quality of life. Another example would be the patient with a hip fracture who, when stable, can be discharged to a skilled nursing facility that provides rehabilitation therapy to receive the services required before being discharged home. As discussed in Chapter 4, the discharge planning manager and the administration together develop new programs of care on site or through joint ventures. The administrator's knowledge of the potential benefits of discharge planning can lead to active support, thereby creating a stronger program.

The patient has the right to be informed and involved in the decision making and planning for posthospital care. The Medicare Quality Protection Act of 1986 (S. 2331 and H.R. 4638), introduced by Senator John Heinz (R-Pa.) and Congressman Pete Stark (D -Calif.), included a section that required discharge planning and viewed it as a quality of care issue.[26] The requirement for hospitals to provide discharge planning, the development of a uniform needs assessment instrument, and the requirement for hospitals to provide a written statement of discharge rights concerning hospital and posthospital care are among the key sections from the

Heinz–Stark Bill included in the Omnibus Budget Reconciliation Act of 1986.[27]

The patient has rights, but how does the patient and the patient's family and significant other view their roles and responsibilities in discharge planning? Part of their responsiblity may fall under the categories of self-care and independence. Self-care focuses on the active consumer interacting with the health care system. The self-care process does ". . .address the goal of enhancing the ability of lay persons to make decisions regarding their health care and also to be able to recognize and exercise options of care."[28] A well-established discharge planning program engages patients and families in identifying the needs and planning for ongoing care. The patient, family, and signficant other must have access to information in order to make informed choices. In a competitive market the assumption is that consumers will be able to make informed choices from among alternatives of care. The forces at play in the health care system will mandate the consumers' participation. With fewer hospital admissions, shorter lengths of stay, more cost sharing, and an increasing elderly population, the question that remains is how consumers will come to understand the issues in order to make appropriate choices.

From the insurers' viewpoint, continuity of care planning provides a mechanism for establishing care utilization at the appropriate level in the appropriate setting. Involvement of insurance companies such as Aetna and Equitable in discharge planning is especially evident with case management, in which potential cases are identified early and alternatives to an acute care setting are explored. The four components of the insurers' case management model are as follows:

1. assessment and planning—determining the patient's condition, and what services and resources are needed;
2. coordination and referral—bringing all the people and services together;
3. patient treatment—dealing with specific medical problems; and
4. continued monitoring—ensuring that all recommendations are being followed and that health is being maintained.[29]

Discharge planners functioning within insurance companies and review organizations are demonstrating the economic advantages of case management. Discharge planners in hospitals have provided insurance companies with data that show the cost savings of home care over prolonged hospital care, as, for example, with ventilator-dependent patients. The role of insurance companies and of businesses that provide health insurance as a benefit to their employees is changing from simply that of payer to that of prudent purchaser of health care services.

The purpose of this chapter was to set the tone and structure for the remainder of the book. The directional forces that affect discharge planning will be expanded on, the principles and practices of discharge planning will be presented from various perspectives, and future issues and strategies will be explored.

NOTES

1. Louise C. Smith, *Factors Influencing Continuity of Nursing Service* (New York: National League for Nursing, 1962).

2. "A Field Nurse for Old Bellevue," *Charities and the Commons* 17 (1906–07): 125.

3. Ida M. Cannon, *Social Work in Hospitals* (New York: Russell Sage Foundation, 1923), p. 14.

4. Smith, *Factors Influencing Continuity of Nursing Service.*

5. Edith Wensley, *Nursing Service Without Walls* (New York: National League for Nursing, 1963), p. 38.

6. Steering Committee of the NLN Division of Nursing, "Statement of Continuity of Nursing Care." August 1966.

7. Linda Nichols and John Feather, "Factors Influencing Discharge Planning Effectiveness and Job Satisfaction," *The Coordinator*, May 1984, pp. 43–45.

8. *Federal Register* 51, no. 116 (Tuesday, June 17, 1986): 22042–52.

9. Dorothy Morgan, "Discharge Planning: An Asset in the Continuum of Patient Care Services," *Canadian Hospital* 50, no. 9 (September 1973): 30.

10. Vicki Previte, "Continuing Care in a Primary Nursing Setting: Role of a Clinical Specialist," *International Nursing Review* 26, no. 2 (1979): 55.

11. Richard C. Edwards, "Professionals in 'Alliance' Achieve More Effective Discharge Planning," *Hospitals* 52 (June 1978): 72.

12. Martha Fortune, "The Role of the Community Health Nursing Consultant in Discharge Planning: Investigating the Possibility." Unpublished report, University of Rochester School of Nursing, 1981.

13. Margaret E. LaMontagne and Kathleen M. McKeehan, "Profile of a Continuing Care Program Emphasizing Discharge Planning," *Journal of Nursing Administration* 5 (1975): 26.

14. Nichols and Feather, "Discharge Planning Effectiveness," pp. 43–45.

15. Harold N. Willard and Stanislaw Kasl, *Continuing Care in a Community Hospital* (Cambridge, Mass.: Harvard University Press, 1972), p. 41.

16. Bernita M. Steffl and Imogene Eide, *Discharge Planning Handbook* (Thorofare, N.J.: Charles B. Slack, 1978).

17. Kathleen M. McKeehan, *Continuing Care, A Multidisciplinary Approach to Discharge Planning* (St. Louis: C. V. Mosby Company, 1981).

18. Public Law 98-21, Title VI. Prospective Payment for Medicare In-Patient Hospital Services. Washington, D.C.: Government Printing Office, 1983.

19. Terrence F. Cahill, "Prospective Reimbursement: Its Effect on Discharge Planning Services," *Discharge Planning Update* 3, no. 1 (Fall 1982): 14–16.

20. _____ "Peer Review Organization (PRO): Medicare and Medicaid Programs," *Discharge Planning Update* 5, no. 1 (Fall 1984): 23.

21. _____ "Professional Review Organizations," *Discharge Planning Update* 5, no. 2 (Winter 1985): 19.

22. _____ "HFCA Lists Questionable Discharges and Transfers as Top PRO Priority," *Discharge Planning Advisor in Hospital Peer Review*, Winter 1986, pp. 4–6.

23. *Information Requirements for Evaluating the Impact of Medicare Prospective Payment on Post-Hospital Long-Term Care Services: Preliminary Report. GAO/PEMD* 85-8 (February 21, 1985): 1–9.

24. Joint Commission on Accreditation of Hospitals, *1987 Accreditation Manual for Hospitals.* (Chicago: author, 1987), SO 21.2.2.3.1, p. 259.

25. Ibid., NR 12.5.5.2, p. 144.

26. The Medicare Quality Protection Act of 1986. Brief Summary of Provisions (June 24, 1986).

27. Conference Report to Accompany H.R. 5300, OBRA of 1986. (October 17, 1986).

28. U.S. Department of Health, Education, and Welfare, *Consumer Self-Care in Health*, NCSHR Research Proceedings Series (Hyattsville, Md.: August 1977).

29. Jackline C. Knable, "Case Management Today and Tomorrow," *Continuing Care Coordinator* April 1986, p. 20.

REFERENCES

Arthur D. Little, Inc. *The Health Care System in the Mid-1990s.* Washington, D.C.: The Health Insurance Association of America, January 1985.

Blendon, R. J. "Health Policy Choices for the 1990s." *Issues in Science and Technology* 11 (Summer 1986): 65–73.

McCall, N.; Rice, T.; and Sangl, J. "Consumer Knowledge of Medicare and Supplemental Health Insurance Benefits." *Health Services Research* 20 (1986): 633–57.

Shamansky, Sherry L.; Boase, Janice C.; and Horn, Beverly M. "Discharge Planning: Yesterday, Today, and Tomorrow." *Home Health Nurse* 14 (May/June 1984): 21.

U.S. General Accounting Office. *Constraining National Health Care Expenditures. GAO/HRD* 85-105, September 30, 1985.

Trends in Health Care and Continuity of Care

Elaine M. Frank

2

A number of forces that affect the health care environment are combining to increase the importance and the need for planning for the continuity of care of patients throughout the health care system. These include demographic changes, epidemiological factors, economic concerns, and political and social changes. This chapter examines some of these factors and their impact on the future of discharge planning.

ECONOMIC FACTORS

The rise in health care costs in excess of the general inflation rate has been recognized as a problem for some time. In 1960 total national health care expenditures were $26.9 billion. By 1984 this figure had increased to $387.4 billion, and by 1986 it was $458 billion. Even more alarming to many is the rise in these costs as a percentage of the gross national product (GNP). In 1960, health care costs accounted for 5 percent of the GNP. By 1984 this figure had doubled to 10.6 percent. By 1986 it had reached 10.9 percent.[1,2] Many separate and interrelated causes have contributed to the increase in health care expenditures.

The implementation of the Medicare and Medicaid programs in the midsixties, along with the increase in the number of Americans covered by some form of private health insurance, brought about a tremendous rise in the availability and accessibility of health care services. As a result, individuals who had previously paid out of pocket for their health care were now covered, to some extent, by a third party payer. These payers, whether public or private, used a retrospective system for reimbursing health care providers. Simply stated, physicians, hospitals, and others provided what they believed was necessary care and were reimbursed accordingly. Health care consumers became distanced from the bills and the bills went up. As costs increased, limits were placed on charges by both the public and the private payers. Copayments and deductibles also rose in an effort to increase consumers' interest in the costs by having them pay a larger share. Contracts with independent review organizations, Professional Standards Review Organizations (PSROs), and then Peer Review Organizations (PROs) were developed to monitor the utilization of health care services. Requirements for second opinions before surgery and other programs to reduce unnecessary procedures were instituted by some insurers. Despite these efforts, health care costs have continued to rise.

The major payers of health care—the federal and state governments and large employers—have been looking at other ways to reduce their costs. One significant approach they have taken is to change to a *prospective* payment system. Examples include Medicare's diagnosis-related group–based system, described in Chapter 1, or any of a variety of capitation plans whereby a provider, like a health maintenance organization (HMO), is paid in advance a set amount per person, regardless of the amount of health care services that are used. Such a system encourages the providers to deliver care as efficiently as possible, since their fees are set in advance and any resulting savings or losses are their own. In this case the provider is said to be at risk. Providers who are reimbursed on a prospective basis have strong incentives to keep down their total costs per patient by keeping their members healthy and by using the most efficient and cost-effective means of providing needed health care when members do become ill.

Some payers are taking another approach. They are controlling the care of those they insure, either directly or indirectly, by requiring preapproval for any procedure or hospitalization. Without this approval no payment will be made to the provider.

Both approaches involve managing the nature of the care a patient receives in an effort to reduce the overall cost of the services, while maintaining the patient at the optimal level of health. This case management approach has changed the view of discharge planning from a luxury to a necessity throughout the health care system.

The concept is based on two premises linking health care costs to the type of care provided. First, there is the recognition that different "levels" or locations of care cost different amounts. Thus an acute hospital stay generally costs more than a nursing home stay, and both are more expensive than home- or community-based services. The other premise is that a person's health care needs may be interrelated with other needs, including economic, social, or psychological needs, and that only by taking a holistic approach to a person's situation can the most efficient treatment method be determined. Further, there is a growing awareness of the connection between a current health care problem and the likelihood of future needs. Thus both providers and payers are moving from an episodic approach to a continuous approach.

Economic pressures to reduce health care costs are bringing about an increased interest in and appreciation of discharge planning for continuity of care.

PAYER CONCERNS

As already mentioned, the pressure to contain health care costs is coming from those who are paying the bills. There are three major groups who currently pay 99 percent of all personal health care expenditures. In 1984 the federal government paid 39.7 percent of all individual health care costs. Private health insurance paid 31.3 percent, and direct payments by individuals accounted for 27.9 percent. The remaining 1.2 percent came from philanthropic sources.[3] The portion attributed to private health insurance reflects the premium payments made by individuals who are insured as well as the share paid by employers. With the growing number of people who are uninsured, the direct payment percentage will probably increase.

Each group is using a variety of techniques to reduce the size of its bill. Several of these techniques merit further explanation.

Both public and private insurance programs have been increasing the percentage of the bill paid directly by consumers by increasing the amount of deductibles and copayments. Although these methods are designed to increase the impact on the consumer of the rising costs of health care, and thus reduce unnecessary utilization, its most direct impact is to shift the burden of costs from third party payers to individuals. For example, in 1985 Medicare recipients paid approximately 16 percent of their total health care costs directly out of pocket. For the first time this represented the same share as older people paid in 1964, when the Medicare program was enacted to reduce the burden of medical bills on the elderly. Another concern stems from the higher share being paid by the insured. For many people these cost increases result in reduced accessibility of health services, which had risen over the past 20 years because of increased public funding. In the long run this reduction may raise the total cost of care by substituting higher-cost care in the future for lower-cost services now.

Another form of cost shifting is, however, being used less than in the past. In less cost-conscious times hospitals and other providers gave the public sector some reductions in its bills and shifted these costs to private insurers. This practice was viewed, by all concerned, as an additional form of social insurance. As employers become increasingly aware of the tremendous amounts being spent on health insurance, however, they are refusing to accept this additional burden and are themselves seeking price reductions from the providers.

Consumers, too, are trying to reduce, or at least gain control over, their costs. There has been, for example, a significant increase in the number of people joining HMOs and other prepaid plans. Such plans have fixed premium fees with few or no additional costs based on the amount of services received. They allow members to know in advance what their health care costs will be. Consumers are also looking for more comprehensive types of insurance and are purchasing additional forms of insurance to fill the gaps in their primary policies. Finally, consumers are demanding that their providers pay attention to cost factors, and are increasingly making at least some decisions based on cost factors, for example, insisting on generic prescriptions and seeking in and out surgery or otherwise substituting ambulatory for inpatient services.

Major employers are perhaps the newest entrants in the cost containment field. Ever since Lee Iacocca announced that health insurance premiums added $500 to the cost of every new Chrysler, big businesses have been paying close attention to this issue. They are seeking the best possible prices from insurance companies and increasingly are negotiating directly with health care providers to get the best deal in health care coverage. More and more they are using "gatekeeping" techniques designed to monitor the necessity of health services before they are used. The term gatekeeping refers to various techniques by which access to health care procedures or providers is controlled. The primary physician traditionally acted as the "gatekeeper" by recommending diagnostics and treatments and through referrals to specialists or particular hospitals. Today third party payers and managed health care systems are becoming more involved in this role.

One of the early gatekeeping techniques to be used was the second opinion, in which a second physician is consulted to corroborate the recommendation of the primary physician. Credited with reducing the number of necessary procedures, second opinions are currently required by many insurers.

The biggest change, however, is in the expanding use of preapprovals for diagnostics as well as for therapeutics. First used by HMOs to eliminate out-of-plan utilization, these programs are now used by many insurers to control the types and the number of procedures being paid for. This technique requires that, except in emergencies, in order to be reimbursable, all tests, treatments, and hospitalizations must be approved in advance.

Another approach is to limit the choice of providers, physicians, hospitals, laboratories, and so forth to those who have agreed to offer the payer price reductions. Preferred Provider Organizations (PPOs) have been established specifically for this purpose. Other payers are adapting the technique to their own situations and needs.

Third party payers are making other changes in how services are reimbursed. These include requiring that certain procedures be carried out on an outpatient basis and reimbursing only for the cost of generic pharmaceuticals.

These gatekeeping techniques offer some benefits, including a reduction in the number of questionably effective treatments and the elimination of some duplication of services. But they are not without costs. Gatekeeping by insurers leads to an erosion in the autonomy of physicians as decision makers and a decline in the choices that consumers have.

DEMOGRAPHIC FACTORS

The most significant demographic trend projected for the near future in terms of its potential impact on U.S. health care is the "graying of America." As a result of advances in both public health and medicine, the average life expectancy of Americans has been increasing. When this trend is combined with rising birth rates, particularly the baby boom after World War II, the projected increase in both the number and the proportion of older people in the population is tremendous.

According to U.S. Census figures, in 1900 those age 65 or over represented 4 percent of the U.S. population. By 1950 this figure had doubled to 8.1 percent. In 1980, 11.3 percent of Americans, or one in nine, were over age 65. Projections indicate that by the year 2000 this figure will have grown to over 13 percent, and somewhere between the years 2020 and 2030, 20 percent of the U.S. population will be over age 65. Even more dramatic is the growth pattern of the segment known as the "old-old," those 85 years of age or over. In 1900 only 0.2 percent of the U.S. population had attained age 85. By 1950 this figure had doubled to 0.4 percent. By 1980, however, the figure had risen to 1 percent, a rise of 250 percent in 30 years. Such a tremendous growth rate has made this segment the fastest growing in our population, and the trend is expected to continue and accelerate. By the year 2020, 2.5 percent of the population is expected to have reached age 85. Beyond that, as the baby boomers become the old-old, the numbers will continue to rise, to reach 5.2 percent by the year 2050.

The aging of the population, particularly the growth in the oldest segment, has tremendous implications for the future in a variety of fields. Of specific interest is its impact on the demand for health services in general and for long-term care and other related services needed by an older population. Another aspect of the aging trend is a reduced demand for those services that are generally associated with a younger population— pediatrics, adolescent medicine, and acute care services in general. In addition, the same advances in medicine that have led to the aging phenomenon have also brought about changes in the delivery mechanisms of health care.

CHANGES IN HEALTH CARE NEEDS

Along with, and to some extent as a direct result of, some of the trends discussed earlier, there are major changes in the nature of the demand for health care and related services. The principal change is a decreased demand for acute inpatient services and an increased need for long-term and community-based chronic care services.

There are several reasons for these changes. The "aging of America" is playing a large role. As more and more people survive to advanced ages, the incidence rate of chronic conditions generally associated with the elderly is increasing. These conditions include arthritis, Alzheimer's disease, renal dysfunction, diabetes, and hypertension. Along with the rise in incidence comes an increased need for long-term care beds, in-home services, outpatient facilities, and other forms of health and human services to treat or maintain persons with these chronic conditions and their resulting functional limitations.

Other contributing factors are the technological improvements in the acute care sector and general advances in medicine. Many people of all ages are surviving accidents and illnesses that, until recently, would have meant certain death. For many of the survivors, however, there remains an ongoing need for services. Several examples illustrate this point. Today a patient with total renal failure not only can survive with this condition, but through either in-home or outpatient services can function very well for many more years. Accident victims who suffer multiple traumatic injuries are often able to recover sufficiently to leave the acute care hospital. For many of them, however, there is an ongoing need for therapy and assistance with personal care. This shift from acute and infectious diseases to long-term chronic conditions is increasing the need for mechanisms to assist and follow patients as they move throughout the health care system.

In addition, the kinds of patients and the chronic care needs that require discharge planning increasingly demand an interaction between the health care and the social service sectors. No longer can these two parts of the human service picture remain distinct. Thus an interdisciplinary approach to discharge planning that addresses both aspects is becoming increasingly essential.

HEALTH CARE PROVIDERS

Changes in who provides health care services and how these services are being provided also play a part in the increased emphasis on discharge planning. In examining the provider issues we must look at providers both as individuals and as organizations.

The major trend in the provision of health care services is the movement toward an integration of services under one provider or among a number of providers forming a coalition of one type or another. The primary impetus for the growth in integrated forms of health care is economic. By sharing some of the facilities and costs involved in the provision of health care, all parties can generally realize savings. Further, by being able to offer a comprehensive approach to health care, the integrated health care provider has an advantage in attracting patients in an increasingly competitive market. This is true for hospitals, nursing homes, and home health agencies as well as for individual physicians.

In order to take advantage of this integration it is essential that patients be transferred from one point in the system to another as efficiently as possible. Their needs must be assessed and a determination made of where within a given system these needs can best be met. Integration further requires that there is an understanding of reimbursement and other regulatory constraints affecting the various levels of care involved, in order that a move can effectively take place without a loss of revenue or inordinate delays. Finally, procedures should be in place that make the move as smooth as possible by maximizing continuity of care and minimizing duplication in both procedures and paperwork. The discharge planning function, if operating properly, can ensure that all of these activities take place, benefiting both the health care providers, who are trying to achieve economic efficiency, and the patients, who should benefit from coordinated and continuous health care services.

As the ratio of physicians to patients grows, physicians must find ways to attract and retain patients. Whereas there was once a shortage of qualified doctors, now there are many indications of a growing surplus in all but the most underserved areas. As a result, many physicians are giving up their individual entrepreneurship to form practice groups, join existing health plans, or arrange other forms of integrated care. Thus, for physicians as well, there is a growing need to implement the discharge planning approach to health care. This allows physicians to follow their patients through the health care system and to ensure that the route is as efficient as possible and that the care at each point is appropriate.

Another provider group undergoing a change in focus is nursing homes. Whereas these long-term care facilities were once both perceptually and in practice "the last stop," they are becoming an integrated part of an expanding continuum of care for geriatric as well as other patients. Because of the additional economic constraints that are being placed on acute care hospitals, more and more patients are being transferred from the hospital to the nursing home for rehabilitation or further stabilization before being discharged to their homes or to community-based living arrangements. For the first time the notion of discharge planning is finding a place in the nursing home, with active plans being made for at least some of the patients from the time they are first admitted.

Generally, as the health care environment changes from one that primarily deals with acute and episodic conditions to one that is increasingly called on to treat chronic conditions, the needs of the providers for channeling and following their patients become clear.Thus discharge planning has become essential for a broad array of health care providers.

HEALTH CARE CONSUMERS

Health care consumers are also becoming increasingly concerned with issues regarding the efficiency and continuity of the care they receive. Part of this increased interest is based on the growing financial role that consumers are playing with regard to their health care. In addition, there is an increased awareness of the rise in health care costs. These economic considerations are leading patients and their families to become more involved in choosing the kinds of services that are needed and where these services should be rendered. For example, with the rise in copayments, many patients are insisting on same-day surgery and other forms of cost savings. To fully realize some of these savings, however, one must have complete information on the availability of a wide variety of services and resources. Because many patients lack knowledge of resources and services, trained case managers provide the necessary information.

In addition to the need for professional expertise is the need to compensate for the interpersonal familiarity between health care provider and patient that has been lost through increased specialization, the rise in group practices, and increased mobility in our society. For many patients there is little, if any, continuity of care as they are transferred from one provider to the next or from one level of care to another. For many there is no one left who they feel knows their case, and thus can advise them on which alternatives are most appropriate.

Finally, the increasing complexity of the health care system and its morass of eligibility guidelines, care guidelines, and other rules for receiving benefits have led many health care consumers to seek health care services that offer them mechanisms to ensure that they do not get lost in the system. Discharge planners who work with consumers and their families as well as with providers can help them make informed decisions.

SUMMARY

The health care environment is affected by a variety of trends. Many of them increase the need for some form of discharge planning or managed care that can help payers, providers, and consumers maximize their resources, ensure the quality of the care being provided, and minimize duplication of services and efforts. In view of these trends, the current growth in the field of discharge planning appears to be only the beginning.

NOTES

1. U.S. General Accounting Office. *Constraining National Health Care Expenditures.* *GAO/HRD* 85-105, September 30, 1985.

2. Division of National Cost Estimate Office of the Actuary Health Care Financing Administration. "National Health Expenditures 1986–2000." *Health Care Financing Review* 8, no. 4 (Summer 1987): 1.

3. U.S. General Accounting Office. *Constraining National Health Care Expenditures.* GAO/HRD 85-105, September 30, 1985.

REFERENCES

Arthur D. Little, Inc. *The Health Care System in the Mid-1990s.* Washington, D.C.: The Health Insurance Association of America, January 1985.

Blendon, R. J. "Health Policy Choices for the 1990s." *Issues in Science and Technology,* Summer 1986, pp. 65–73.

Blendon, R. J., and Altman, D. E. "Public Attitudes About Health-Care Costs: A New

Lesson in National Schizophrenia." *New England Journal of Medicine* 311, no. 9 (1984): 613–16.

Congressional Clearinghouse on the Future. *Tomorrow's Elderly: Issues for Congress*. Washington, D.C.: Congressional Institute for the Future, 1985.

Health Care Financing Administration. *Long-Term Care: Background and Future Directions*. HCFA 81-20047. Washington, D.C., 1981.

Tyson, K. W., and Merrill, J. C. "Health Care Institutions: Survival in a Changing Environment." *Journal of Medical Education* 59 (1984): 773–82.

U.S. Bureau of the Census. "Population Estimates and Projections." Current Population Reports, Series p-25, No. 922. Washington, D.C.: Government Printing Office, 1984.

Part II

The Discharge Planning Program

Chapter 3

Essential Considerations in Setting Up a Discharge Planning Program

Margaret A. Terry

3

Establishing and managing a discharge planning program challenges the skills of even the most seasoned manager. Success depends on many factors. Awareness of these factors will enhance program development and lay the foundation for an effective program.

The manager responsible for program development has the difficult task of bringing together coalitions of professionals to plan for an individual patient's discharge. Frequently these alliances must be developed in spite of hospital organizational structures.

The discharge planning program must be designed to assure efficiency and control. On the other hand, participation and cooperation are required from the diverse disciplines to bring the available expertise to each patient's discharge plan.

A knowledge of the internal organizational structures, operations, and priorities is a prerequisite if the manager is to succeed in getting professionals and departments to focus on the common goal of effective discharge planning. In addition, the manager needs to be fluent in the regulatory and reimbursement issues that affect all of health care. Also, an understanding of other health care organizations' priorities is necessary so that effective affiliations can be developed.

Other factors and issues to which the manager must direct attention in setting up and developing discharge planning programs are as follows:

- The need for cooperation from diverse disciplines that do not report to the discharge planning program manager and require incentives for involvement
- The need for active involvement and decision making from patients and families who have little understanding of the system and are coping with major financial and personal decisions

- The need for information, support, and cooperation from physicians who do not understand the process and have time constraints, and who are confused about their role in discharge planning
- The lack of reimbursed and affordable community-based services
- The need to work with community-based programs and agencies that have complex eligibility requirements and, frequently, long delays in processing paperwork
- A changing regulatory and reimbursement health care environment that mandates earlier institutional discharges for financial survival
- The need for efficiency in designing systems to target patients who would benefit most

These factors need to be taken into consideration as a program is structured within each organization. This chapter outlines strategies and approaches for addressing these issues and minimizing inherent problems.

ADMINISTRATIVE SUPPORT

One of the most significant factors in establishing a successful discharge planning program is the support of administration. As in all organizations, the executive level sets the tone and fosters a sense of commitment to the program's ideals and goals. As health care organizations become more complex and multilayered, the commitment to this particular program, discharge planning, becomes more essential.

Discharge planners who responded in the comprehensive study done by John Feather and Linda Nichols of 200 U.S. hospitals cited administrative support as crucial. They believed that the relationship between the discharge planners and the rest of the hospital, specifically the support and cooperation of the hospital adminstration, was most closely associated with effective discharge planning.[1]

Discharge planning is the assessment of individual client needs, and the obtaining and coordinating of services and resources. Each stage of this process requires effective communication and cooperation among all disciplines within one's organization.

Hosptials traditionally are organized and managed along professional and departmental lines, including medical, nursing, ancillary, social, dietary, housekeeping, and other services. In addition, physicians present a unique challenge as nonemployees who are nevertheless in control of the patient's care. In theory and on organizational charts, every hospital activity is accountable to the patient and, in a managerial sense, to the governing board.

As a practical matter, the compartmentalized nature of hospital organizations, coupled with professional jealousies and turf battles, impedes multidisciplinary communication and cooperation and efficient management of patient care. To overcome departmental and professional barriers, administration needs to send a clear message that this program is a top priority and that cooperation is expected.

Hospital administrators need to review organizational structures and their reporting systems to assure integration and collaboration of those departments most involved in discharge planning. The development of incentives and rewards to overcome these barriers must be explored. Some specific measures that administration could implement to encourage cooperation and ensure coordination are mandatory attendance at weekly discharge planning meetings, patient care conferences, and review of patients and cases with the utilization review, quality assurance, and admission departments.

Incentives for physician involvement can be accomplished through the monitoring of physician activity by way of the hospital's quality assurance program. Well-organized quality assurance programs that provide standards for physician practice and monitoring and that possess authority within the medical staff structure are essential for successful discharge planning.

As stated in Chapter 1, health care administrators must understand the necessity for and the benefits of an effectively run program. By knowing the potential financial gains, the potential effect on the quality of patient care, and other planning issues, an administrator can create hospitalwide incentives and rewards for all disciplines engaged in the discharge planning program.

TYPES OF ORGANIZATIONAL STRUCTURES

Discharge planning programs in hospitals come in many shapes and forms. Some hospitals choose to assign the functioning role to the primary nurse at the bedside, others choose to make this the sole responsibility of the social work department, while others have an elaborate structure of team participation with shared responsibilities.

The literature cites numerous articles that examine effective approaches to discharge planning. One model is described by Clausen in her article "Staff RN: A Discharge Planner for Every Patient." In this model the central coordinator of the program is the staff nurse. Clausen's concern is that "discharge planning stands in jeopardy of being left to everyone's discretion, and therefore, to no one's accountability."[2] These staff nurses then work with a multidisciplinary task force composed of social workers, dietitians, chaplains, physical and occupational therapists, and other nurses. A discharge planning coordinator is assigned to teach discharge planning skills to all nurses, act as a resource, and build ties with community resources.

Another model is described by Edwards and involves a program built on an alliance of social workers and registered nurse patient care coordinators. The components of the program include identification, needs assessment, service coordination, and follow-up. The program includes weekly meetings.[3]

Reichelt and Newcomb surveyed 14 Chicago hospitals and describe four models of discharge planning.[4] The first model is the most structured and involves a designated discharge planner (usually a nurse), who has clear responsibility to determine what services the patient may need beyond the hospitalization period. This person is an independent agent, selecting and assessing patient needs. A second model is a variation on the first, in which the nursing and medical staff identify patients with needs and then consult the discharge planner for assistance in determining appropriate services. A third model designates discharge planning activities to specific people. Nurses and social workers assigned to units collaborate on a day-to-day basis and screen patients for posthospitalization needs. Then discharge planning activities are divided between nursing and social services, according to whether home care or nursing home placement referral is needed. In the fourth model the social service department receives requests for patient assistance from medicine and nursing and coordinates all discharge planning activities.

In the study cited earlier, which involved 226 discharge planners, Feather and Nichols hoped to be able to reflect discharge planning activities across the country. Their findings revealed that almost half (46 percent) of all discharge planners belong to multidisciplinary teams; half the planners are social workers and a fourth are nurses.[5] Many diverse models can exist for a successful program as long as several crucial elements are present. As with any program, one must look to the existing institutional resources, strengths, and limitations before development can begin.

DEVELOPMENT OF A CENTRALIZED PROGRAM

A discharge planning program must be developed around centralized responsibilities and decentralized involvement. The ideal organizational structure would be a department with a director at the department head level within a hospital; this department would include representation from both nursing and social work. Programs that are managed by a multidisciplinary team whose individual members have diverse priorities and complex reporting mechanisms are less effective. The centralized responsibility for the development, management, and evaluation of a discharge planning program must clearly rest within one department.

Decentralized involvement refers to the intervention and interaction of multiple disciplines in the assessment, diagnosis, planning, and implementation of individual patient discharge planning.

Important centralized components include involvement and responsibility sharing by the key disciplines of nursing and social work. Nursing's involvement recognizes the quicker-and-sicker nature of patients leaving the hospital today. Nurses must be part of discharge planning in order to assess the medical and nursing needs of patients, to discuss and alert physicians about the various levels of care and sites available, and to coordinate the detailed and technical services needed by these patients.

The participation of the discharge planning nurse occurs, for example, when patients are leaving the hospital on nutritional support, such as hyperalimentation. For home hyperalimentation the nurse will need to arrange for (a) the feeding formula to be obtained and delivered; (b) the home skilled-nursing follow-up for the provision and monitoring of parenteral feedings; (c) the necessary teaching for the patient and family about the management of all aspects of possible home complications and whom to contact; (d) the medical monitoring by physicians; and (e) the laboratory monitoring. This one highly technical and complex discharge planning situation must be developed and planned for with an awareness of the other needs and resources available to the patient. The linkage between social work and nursing is essential to efficiently and comprehensively plan for patients' discharge needs.

The social work responsibility focuses on the development of a psychosocial assessment for each patient and family and the offering of supportive counseling to the patient, the family, and significant others. In response to the recognition of the emotional, social, and financial consequences of disabling, sudden, and chronic illnesses to patient and family systems, social workers bring special skills and expertise in psychosocial assessment and intervention, as well as their knowledge of financial and community resources, to patients leaving the hospital. Strong social work linkages with community resources allow for timelier and more appropriate referrals that are tailored to the unique needs of each case.

A centralized program is essential for staying abreast of a changing and regulatory environment. The importance of understanding these changes can best be demonstrated through an examination of related home health care issues.

A number of reimbursement and regulatory changes have recently impacted on the home health care industry. These changes have led home health agencies to be more careful when selecting potential patients. Understanding some of the subtle changes, such as the current definitions of "skilled care" and "homebound," requires frequent and current contact with these agencies. Most astute health care professionals are aware that service availability is frequently reimbursement-dependent. With the regulatory and reimbursement environment constantly changing, organizations can effectively plan for aftercare only when it is the responsibility of a centralized staff.

Staying current on funding levels and service availability requires a centralized discharge planning staff. Many community-based chronic care programs are funded either through government agencies, such as the Area Agency on Aging, or by private foundations. Availability of certain services or nursing home beds is a constantly changing situation that frequently requires a response within hours or the resource is lost.

The dialogue between the hospital discharge planning program and community resources needs to be continuous. Centralization of a department and a division allows the continuous exchange of information among health care professionals and the other organizations. Designating one or two persons as liaison workers to exclusively work with these specific resources enhances the efficiency of this communication. It also capitalizes on the informal contacts and relationships that are essential between organizations. Assuring accessibility of the staff to community agencies prevents the loss of resources and allows the entire department to remain up to date on program changes. This can be accomplished by limiting liaison workers' responsibilities with case assignments. Major responsibilities should be to coordinate community resources with patient and family needs once they are identified by other staff members.

The last element provided by a centralized program is a systematic approach to discharge planning. Such an approach permits assessment, planning, implementation, and evaluation of each patient's discharge plan as well as evaluation of the overall program for the hospital or multicorporate system. A centralized program becomes responsible for the patient's movement through the health care system.

DEVELOPMENT OF A PROGRAM WITHOUT A CENTRALIZED STRUCTURE

Discharge planners who attempt to develop a program either with limited economic resources or at smaller institutions confront similar issues but different approaches.

The sole discharge planner, whether nurse or social worker, must define his or her role. The inherent dilemma in this position is that there are too many issues and problems and not enough time. The discharge planner must primarily be a program coordinator and secondarily be a patient care coordinator. Others must be relied on to assist in the discharge planning process.

The program coordinator must take the following approaches:

- Set program goals and direction.
- Actively involve other disciplines and define their program involvement.
- Focus on the broader issues that affect the program, such as regulatory and reimbursement changes.
- Develop and maintain contacts with community organizations.
- Recognize the limitations of your skills and use the skills of other disciplines when appropriate.
- Develop power and influence in your organization and learn to use it (see Chapter 4 for further discussion).
- Establish guidelines defining patients for whom the discharge planner will do discharge planning.

INVOLVEMENT OF OTHER DISCIPLINES

Involving key disciplines early in the planning stages fosters a sense of commitment to the program's goals. By bringing its professional philosophies and priorities to the planning process, each discipline will also shape and design a program reflective of the comprehensive approach needed in discharge planning. In addition, the professionals will have an opportunity to define their involvement and roles in the new program. Early participation can be the key to establishing a future of cooperation, collaboration, and communication.

Once the program has been established, future participation can take place on different levels. Most discharge planning programs call for weekly meetings to be held on patient care units within the hospital. These meetings are frequently multidisciplinary and bring together the disciplines that are essential to individual patient care planning. They also provide comprehensive information about each patient to all disciplines that are involved in the aftercare planning.

Another forum through which other departments and disciplines may participate is formal meetings with representation from the discharge planning department, the utilization review or quality assurance department, the financial counseling or patient accounts department, and the admissions department. This group's purpose is twofold: to highlight the patients with the most complicated discharge planning needs and to share information to facilitate appropriate decision making.

Once the program is operational, representatives from key disciplines— respiratory, occupational, speech, and physical therapy; social work, dietary, nursing, and utilization review departments; hospital administration; and medicine—can establish a discharge planning committee. The committee's role would be to share information on federal and state regulatory changes, discuss financial implications, and survey resource and service availability.

The committee would also examine internal communications to assure effective integration of all disciplines. In addition, it would provide ongoing input to the program and create a sense of ownership for the disciplines involved in the process. Keeping this committee updated on the important statistics that reflect the program's impact is essential. The data should include average lengths of stay, number of patients awaiting nursing home placement, number of patients referred and placed in nursing homes and personal care facilities, and number of referrals to home health agencies. Ongoing evaluation and reshaping of the discharge planning program are necessary to reflect changing priorities in the health care environment. The strategy of including key professionals in overall program evaluation is essential to the enhancement of cooperation in a centralized program.

THE NEW TEAM APPROACH

Multidisciplinary team work has been the professed and accepted mode for performing the discharge planning function. The virtues of assessing and providing care in this mode have been lauded by all in the discharge planning arena. The approach seems to be based on the desire to take into account complex and highly technical needs, to evaluate the whole person, and to use the expertise of the many professionals at hand.

Congruent with the previous discussion, which supported a centralized program and decentralized involvement, the approach that best meets today's needs is a hybrid. It is a case management approach by a single discharge planner with a multidisciplinary team of professionals in consultation. Most discharge planning programs have charged a discharge planner—nurse, social worker, or other health professional—with the responsibility of coordinating the discharge plan. The discharge planner needs to assess, coordinate, and implement a plan for each patient's needs.

This must be accomplished through constant input from the participating disciplines. The approach recognizes that at times, other disciplines, because of their expertise, may provide most of the significant discharge planning. This position must rest in a department within the institution that has the overall responsibility for the program.

To gain a greater understanding of why a case management team input approach is most effective, it is necessary to look at the functions of the discharge planner. First, the discharge planner must make an assessment based on the medical, nursing, and social status of the patient. This activity frequently requires the professional input of nurses, therapists, physicians, social workers, and other health care providers. Functional abilities before admission, during hospitalization, and at discharge are also assessed. Next the discharge planner is required to have a thorough knowledge of programs in the community, funding sources, eligibility criteria, and the patient's needs. The discharge planner is then faced with the task of determining the patient's and family's support system and their ability to deal with this situation. This determination can be based on an assessment by a social worker or other health care professional. Lastly, the discharge planner needs to be able to bring patients and families to an informed decision as quickly as possible. These activities require individual decision making as well as input from multiple disciplines.

Today's discharge planner is working in an environment of significantly shortened lengths of stay in hospitals and other health care settings. Health care organizations, patients, and families face tremendous financial liability for a prolonged length of stay. The case manager or discharge planning modality offers the most efficient approach to responsible coordination of posthospital care.

What can be designed to simultaneously ensure the timely and multiple input of professionals to the discharge plan and the patient's and family's informed decision making? One method has been the implementation of predischarge planning rounds held weekly on each patient unit, followed by the more in-depth and formal multidisciplinary discharge planning meeting. Weekly predischarge planning rounds are attended by the discharge planner and the head or assistant head nurse, and accomplish the task of screening all patients on the unit to ascertain current function status, future prognosis, and family and social situation. Such rounds provide the discharge planner with initial information to start charting a plan for the patient's future needs. Through this process the discharge planner determines if an in-depth assessment should be done and if the patient should be reviewed at the formal weekly discharge planning meeting. This multidisciplinary meeting provides each professional with comprehensive information on the patient's current and future needs so that appropriate care can be provided. Documentation of these meetings in each patient's medical record and documentation of follow-up activity by each discipline provide ongoing and current information. This information is accessible to the discharge planner and others involved in providing patients and families with accurate and up-to-date information in the course of establishing and working toward timely and appropriate discharge plans.

The discharge planning meeting is the starting point of all future collaboration and communication among the professionals involved in the discharge planning process. Through the formal discharge planning meetings and the less formal team discussions, staff nurses will become aware of potential discharge dates and of family members who will participate in the home care arrangements. With this data, patient educational programs and other activities can be tailored to meet each patient's specific needs.

In today's hospitals and other health care organizations, teams of professionals have been established to attend to the complex needs of patients with special problems. The team modality seems best suited to these groups of patients who have highly technical and complex care problems. Such patients often have long lengths of stay and can benefit from the closely coordinated attention of the professionals at hand. Examples of these specialized teams or units are the geriatric assessment team or unit, the nutritional support team, and the rehabilitation team or unit. In circumstances where such specialized teams exist, the discharge planner's role is still to assume the primary responsibility for discharge planning. The discharge planner needs to be part of these teams to assure that all discharge planning needs are assessed and acted on, not just those that relate to the team's special interest.

Teamwork is most successful when the team shares a common purpose, the roles of the individual members are clearly differentiated, and the communication process is clearly delineated. Teams work best when the same people work together over a period of time to develop the needed respect and rapport. Specialized teams are better suited to today's health care environment because they encompass few disciplines, see a limited number of patients with potentially long lengths of stay, and have a specific purpose. The discharge planner's challenge is to obtain input from the more traditionally involved disciplines and to work with these new teams to coordinate the entire continuing care plan for the patient and family and the health care organization.

Discharge planning managers are confronted with several challenges to facilitate effective communication. They must develop routine procedures for recordkeeping and in-hospital interdisciplinary communication, as well as assure the transfer of information to other providers so that they will have an accurate and up-to-date data base.

PROFESSIONAL TURF ISSUES

The turf issues in discharge planning are mostly between the disciplines of nursing and social work. The literature contains many articles that discuss effective approaches to the discharge planning function, with either discipline managing the process. For discharge planning to be effective, both professions must collaborate. The optimum organizational structure to facilitate the linkage between nursing and social work is to house both disciplines within the same department. One discipline, though, must be assigned the primary responsibility for managing the discharge planning program. The same discipline must also be responsible for the screening function.

To decide which discipline should have the primary responsibility for managing the program, one must look first at the tasks that must be accomplished and the knowledge and skills required to do so. All the tasks described in Table 3-1 can be accomplished by either discipline for uncomplicated cases. Because of the educational preparation and skills of each discipline, though, each is better suited for different functions. There must be a mechanism in the program to involve the appropriate discipline when a situation becomes too complex for the primary discipline to handle.

To accomplish these tasks there needs to be acceptance of each discipline's expertise and active cooperation to involve the appropriate discipline when needed. A collaborative relationship is essential for an effective and efficient discharge planning program.

PHYSICIAN'S ROLE

The physician's role in discharge planning in the past and, to a lesser extent, the present has been that of gatekeeper to the health care system. Physicians frequently coordinate services for their patients when their patients receive services from other physicians or when patients are receiving radiology or laboratory testing. The literature since the late 1970s reflects the difficulty faced by consumers when several physicians were involved in their care. The increased number of family practice residencies is a response to the need for a primary care physician who is aware of all the issues.

Table 3-1 Knowledge and Skills for Discharge Planning Management

Tasks to Be Accomplished	Knowledge and Skills Needed
Screening and casefinding	Requires knowledge of those patients with complicated illnesses and needs and an efficient mechanism to identify those patients. Either discipline can effectively perform this task.
Patient assessment	Requires the skills to review a patient's chart, assess current and future medical, nursing, and social needs and involve relevant disciplines. This requires nursing's participation. For some patients in the acute care setting, as well as patients in institutions and agencies of a less acute level of care, other disciplines such as social work can assess needs.
Assist patient and family in decision-making process	Human relation skills to assist patient and family to make an informed decision. In-depth problems such as family conflict, depression, or unrealistic expectations of self or patient require an understanding of the dynamics of human behavior. Social work participation is essential.
Planning, implementing, and coordinating	Communication and assertiveness skills are required. A thorough knowledge of patient needs is essential. Nursing or social work, depending on patient situation and needs, can perform this task.
Ability to obtain financial assistance	Knowlege of private and government insurers, of income levels for state medical assistance programs, special pharmacy assistance programs, etc. Social work has primary responsibility. Nursing must also be knowledgeable.
Referral to other appropriate services and institutions, i.e., nursing homes, home health agencies, homemaker services, durable medical equipment companies	Knowledge of programs and qualifying criteria of agencies or institutions to include medical, nursing, and financial knowledge. Referrals to nursing homes are handled best by both disciplines jointly, home health agencies by nursing, and homemaker and equipment services by either discipline. For rehabilitation equipment, a physical, occupational, or speech therapist must be consulted.

When moving from the arena of coordinating medical services for a patient to coordinating community-based services, the physician faces even more difficulty. Physicians with the best of intentions cannot be expected to know the availability of services and the eligibility requirements for these services. Nevertheless, the physician's signature has been required for patients to receive reimbursement of services. Physicians are often expected to initiate, take responsibility for, and ratify the actions of all other providers in the health care system. In this country, where the medical model for health care delivery is dominant, the physician's signature becomes a passport for patients to receive reimbursed services in hospitals, nursing homes, and the home setting. Under this medical model, federal and state governments as well as private insurers frequently require the physician's order or signature to sanction the need for community-based services.

A role for physicians in discharge planning can only be achieved when physicians understand the complexity of the issues, the knowledge base and skills needed, and the enormous amount of time required. For example, physicians must be willing to recognize that an elderly patient might be admitted to the hospital because he or she has a number of medical and functional problems. The physician is skilled in managing the patient's congestive heart failure and renal problems but needs to comprehend that this patient might not be able to return home because of functional and family support problems. The astute physician will recognize such patients early and refer them to the appropriate hospital or institutional discharge planner so that an evaluation of the patient's needs can begin.

In today's environment, physicians still determine when patients are hospitalized and when they are discharged. But the process is complicated by new regulations that determine what is an appropriate hospitalization and an appropriate length of stay. The payers of service have forced hospitals to set up elaborate admission screening procedures and more complicated discharge planning programs. The physician's role thus becomes more circumscribed, primarily focusing on the medical management of the patient. Key roles for the physicians in discharge planning include supporting the discharge planning process, actively predicting patients' medical needs, and, most important, encouraging patients and families to realistically begin planning for the future.

To enlist and encourage physician support, discharge planning managers need to keep physicians informed of the progress of their patients' discharge plans. Minimizing paperwork, providing timely follow-through, and establishing professional credibility are essential strategies to enlist physicians' cooperation.

In today's hospital when patients' lengths of stay are incorporated into criteria for evaluating physicians' practices, well-managed discharge planning programs are a welcome resource to the physician.

Discharge planning managers, since the prospective payment system, have new leverage in working with physicians. Because hospitals are financially affected by long lengths of stay, discharge planning managers can now work with utilization or quality assurance departments when physicians' actions are delaying discharge procedures. Discharge planners also act on behalf of a patient to delay a potential discharge when the patient is not medically able to go to the aftercare setting.

Working within the organized structure of the medical staff, the discharge planning manager needs to set up cooperative procedures to ensure physicians' cooperation at the appropriate time. One effective approach to assure immediate physician response is to enlist cooperation through the physician chairman. These physicians participate in developing hospital policy and are responsible for assuring quality care within their practice area. Procedures can be developed within the discharge planning department in cooperation with the physician chairman to provide the planner with appropriate support at crucial times.

Another approach would be to work with the physician advisers in the quality assurance program. As active members of the medical staff, physicians review other physicians' activities to assure acceptable standards. When a problem occurs the physician adviser calls the physician to discuss other approaches. Mechanisms are in place for a second physician adviser review if an agreement is not reached.

But just when physicians are becoming aware of the benefits of discharge planning, fewer patients are being admitted to the hospital.

The dilemma for physicians and patients alike is the lack of support in the community to assist them in obtaining coordinated care. The need for a continuum-of-care program within the community is evident.

INSURER'S ROLE

Both the government and private insurers are redefining the way that health care services are paid for and delivered. The government, private payers, and health maintenance organizations have moved from the role of paying for services to deciding the appropriateness of services and to designating which particular company, agency, or institution will provide that service. The payers for health services are becoming prudent buyers, attempting to purchase the best service at the lowest cost. Decisions today are largely based on costs, not necessarily on an evaluation of the quality of care available. Decisions based on quality are difficult to make, since the definitions remain unclear. What is so new and different about this change is that the consumer and the physician will have fewer choices in the future. Because of the spiraling cost of health care over the past decade, private insurers and the government have responded differently to this problem.

Owing to the demands from the business community for cost containment, private insurers are contracting with providers for discounted services. Employees of these companies are being channeled into using designated providers.[6] This active role by the insurers is even more evident for employees who are in the category of high users of medical care. In this situation, consultants are used to assist the client in finding the best, most cost-effective method of care. U.S. Corporate Health Management found that at one corporation, between 3 percent and 4 percent of the employees ran up 40 percent of the health care costs.[7] Those are the employees that the management firms are addressing. This approach is known as case management and is offered to employees who have serious illnesses, such as cancer, stroke, or heart disease.

The case management approach is significant for two reasons: First, it reflects a shift in responsibility for coordination and decision making on care options away from the patient, physician, and hospital discharge planner to the payers; second, the choice of providers is frequently limited to those designated by the insurers. Discharge planning for continuity of care takes on a new phase in these arrangements, with coordination being done by those who are most concerned with the cost of services. Patients, families, and physicians may be given options, but unless the patient chooses those prescribed by the case management programs, one choice comes with a higher price tag than another. Discharge planners need to be aware of the nature of case management programs. In working with the insurers, planners need to clarify the roles of these case managers in the hospital. Once responsibilities have been delineated, the planners need to explore and inform patients and families of the options available. The obvious response of the government to spiraling health care costs has been Medicare's prospective payment reimbursement system. Under this program, hospitals are paid a fixed rate based on the diagnostic-related group (DRG), thereby creating incentives to decrease lengths of stay.

Through this fixed-rate reimbursement and the Peer Review Organization's new admission criteria, Medicare patients are admitted to the hospital for fewer diagnoses and shorter periods.

Discharge planning programs have been given more support and attention because of these changes. Managing these programs, however, requires more skill and organization to respond to the new demands to responsibly discharge patients sooner.

Medicare's approach to control costs in home health care has been done through "administrative actions designed to restrict services and undercut the benefits promised under Medicare Law."[8]

Most significant are the new guidelines and policy directives that define homebound and intermittent skilled care. These two qualifying criteria have been interpreted more restrictively by many fiscal intermediaries. Home health agencies are thus more selective in accepting certain clients. These new restrictions further limit reimbursed home care options for the elderly and the disabled. This forces planners to look to non-Medicare payment sources or out-of-pocket costs for patients. The ultimate effect is that those who are unable to pay privately frequently have no community-based options.

SCREENING AND CASEFINDING

The first step in the discharge planning process is the identification of patients who would require assistance as they moved from one health care setting to the next. As in previous sections of this chapter, the hospital will be used as the model to describe this activity. The model and concepts described here can be applied to other health care settings. Before setting up screening and casefinding mechanisms the goals of this function need to be established.

Hospitals have traditionally identified high-risk groups of patients. High-risk patients, for the purposes of discharge planning, are those who will require in-depth assessment and a coordinated approach to their health care needs before they are discharged. The assumptions have been made that these identified groups of patients could not safely leave the hospital when medically stable unless services were in place for them. Criteria such as age, diagnosis, family and living arrangements, and a combination of social, medical, and emotional factors have been used to place patients in these high-risk categories.

The standard screening criteria have become antiquated with the changes in reimbursement for hospitalization. Hospitals must be ready to move patients to the next care setting when patients become medically stable. In addition, hospitals must respond to the constantly shifting definition of medically stable.

Institutions that are aggressively trying to survive in this new financial climate will not passively wait for patients to become medically stable, but will set up programs to identify patients who can receive high-technology services in another setting, such as the home. Screening takes on heightened importance in this new financial environment because early identification now is essential when average lengths of stay have been reduced to seven or eight days. Screening also takes on a new dimension owing to the increasing number of patients who will need to be screened. Many patients will need to receive post-hospitalization services while they continue their recovery from an acute episode. Exhibit 3-1 incorporates

Exhibit 3-1 Discharge Planning Screening Tool

Criteria for Identifying Patients with Potential Discharge Planning Needs

- Activities of daily living dependent (patients who need assistance with ADLs)
- Age (65 +, especially those 75 +)
- Diagnosis with long-term consequences (cancer, stroke, chronic renal failure, diabetes, chronic obstructive pulmonary disease, congestive heart failure)
- Intravenous therapy (patients primarily hospitalized to receive antibiotics, hyperalimentation)
- Lack of consciousness or orientation (comatose, lethargic, disoriented, etc.)
- Living arrangement problems (lived alone, or previous situation is inadequate)
- Medications (new to insulin injections, non-compliance, multiple medications)
- Nursing home, personal care home, or community facility (patient from other facility)
- Nutritional support (patients receiving tube feeding, etc.)
- Ostomies (new colostomy, ileostomy)
- Rehabilitation (patient receiving physical, occupational, or speech therapy)
- Respirator (patients on respirator not in intensive care unit)
- Tubes in place (Foley, tracheostomy, suprapubic, gastrostomy, nasogastric)

---

the traditional screening criteria with high-technology categories into a new discharge planning screening tool.

This new regulatory and financial environment for hospitals means that fewer patients will be admitted to the hospital for care and that many patients will need linkages with community resources after in-and-out surgery visits, out-patient treatments, and emergency department visits.

In establishing the screening and casefinding function of the discharge planning program, one must look to existing organizational structures, forms, and processes. For example, if the admissions department produces a daily list of admissions, that list provides basic data for screening. Existing procedures can frequently be amended or computerized information reprogrammed to meet the needs of other departments, such as discharge planning. Major changes in programming might require additional administrative support. Some hospitals require preadmission screening, which is done through the utilization review or admissions department. This department frequently has information that will alert the discharge planner to patients who are going to need coordinated discharge planning. In most hospitals today, planned admissions are preregistered in advance, and therefore the admissions department has data on patients who are scheduled to be admitted for planned surgery or medical workups. This often can be a source of information for the discharge planner.

These initial screening processes are helpful only with the traditionally high-risk patients. Under the new regulatory and financial environment, discharge planners must screen all patients to identify those who might benefit from high-technology services so that they can be discharged earlier. The goal of screening and casefinding is to try to make an early identification of patients who need discharge planning. The traditional method for screening patients used by most hospitals is the multidisciplinary discharge planning—nursing unit rounds, or patient care rounds. At such meetings a brief description can be given of all patients on that particular unit with a further in-depth assessment by the discharge planner at a later time. The initial screening consists of a review of all patients with the nursing staff. This review appropriately identifies patients to be discussed in a multidisciplinary meeting. After the initial review a list of patients to be discussed in more detail is posted on the patient care unit.

TEAM MEETINGS

The multidisciplinary meeting is subsequently held with representation from the appropriate professionals. This provides for a more in-depth discussion of the identified patients.

The weekly meetings on each patient care unit need to be held at the same specified time and to be well structured so that expectations are clear for all involved. Keeping the meeting to a time limit, such as 1 hour, is important.

Providing the nursing staff as well as other professionals with a list of information to bring makes the meeting more consistent and meaningful, and assists the "new" nurse or part-time nurse with this role expectation. Exhibit 3-2 shows what information the nursing staff should bring to the discharge planning meeting.

With this method of review, the discharge planner can identify those patients who have specific diagnoses or treatment needs for which an early discharge to an alternative setting might be arranged.

Because the discharge planner looks to all professionals who have contact with the patient and family as potential sources of referrals, it is important to have high visibility within the hospital setting. Beside physicians, nursing staff are the key professionals making referrals. Nursing staff, through their admission nursing assessment, are in an excellent position to assess patients' current functional status compared with their functional status before admission. In setting up the program it is essential

Exhibit 3-2 Nursing Staff Information List for Discharge Planning Meetings

Patient identifying information (name, room number, age)
Date of admission and reason for admission
Arrangements before admission
Present and past diagnoses
Reason for referral to discharge planning
Living arrangement, e.g., lives alone
Support system, e.g., daughter, husband
Current activities of daily living
   Eating
   Bathing and dressing
   Mobility, e.g., wheelchair, bed rest
   Bladder and bowel control
   Level of consciousness
Activities of daily living before admission
Skin integrity (describe)
I.V. meds and purpose
Treatments
Rehabilitation (physical, occupation, or speech therapy)
Stability of condition
Other pertinent information, e.g., lab, x-ray
Anticipated teaching or service needs before discharge

to review the nursing admission data base to ensure inclusion of key questions. The following information can be obtained by the nursing staff:

- Place of residence (nursing home, home, senior housing, etc.)
- Supportive people available to patient
- People at home who require care
- Services and equipment in home (nurse, homemaker, social worker, wheelchair, etc.)
- Preadmission activities of daily living (ambulation, dressing, feeding, etc.)

This information can be summarized in a note that contains some basic information about the patient at the time of admission. As the nursing staff becomes intimately involved in discharge planning, this information becomes more relevant and the nursing staff becomes the key ally to accomplish discharge planning.

PREADMISSION AND OUTPATIENT

The key to a successful discharge planning program is to identify as early in the hospitalization as possible those patients who would benefit from the program. Hospital preadmission discharge planning is one way of achieving this goal. Through the use of surgical posting lists and hospital preregistration and waiting lists for planned admissions the discharge planner can review the information available and call patients and families to discuss potential problems. This method has been effective for families when they are aware that patients might need a nursing home placement or follow-up services post hospitalization. Because many hospitals require preadmission testing, making information available, within the preadmission testing center, about the discharge planning department is another way to reach patients with potential care needs.

With fewer patients being admitted, hospitals have a responsibility to assist patients at other points of contact, such as the emergency department or in-and-out surgery units.

To address the discharge planning needs of these specialty areas requires some research and trial. In the case of the emergency department, the manager needs to know patient volumes and specifics about the patients, such as age, diagnosis, and percentage admitted to the hospital. A review of patient charts might provide the manager with some basic data to begin. In the in-and-out surgery unit, knowledge of the diagnostic procedures performed and of the volumes will enable the discharge planning manager to estimate coverage needs.

Educational programs for the staff in both these areas are essential to facilitate referrals to discharge planning. Contact with these departments on a regular basis, such as three times a week, also provides the high visibility needed to remind the staff of planning for the patient's needs.

ROLE OF THE PATIENT AND FAMILY IN DECISION MAKING

- Consumers will be increasingly responsible for their own care.
- As consumers pay more of the cost they will become more interested in its efficient management and will relinquish some of their past autonomy in support of more cost-effective care.
- There will be more health care services for the aged.

- By the mid 1990s or earlier there will be intense public pressure for protection against the cost of long-term care.
- The shift of care from inpatient to ambulatory setting will accelerate.
- Health care will increasingly be delivered within managed systems.
- Population mobility and increased physician specialization have rendered obsolete the ideal of a long-term relationship with the family physician who provides most of the care a patient needs.[9]

These statements, taken from a study by Arthur D. Little, Inc., titled *The Health Care System in the Mid 1990s*, predict the impact of the health care system on consumers. To understand the role of the patient and family in the decision-making process we need to reflect on these statements.

In discharge planning the involvement of patient and family in decision making has traditionally been seen as key to the acceptance of and compliance with any plans.

Given the predictions for the future, we need to look at the kinds of choices consumers will realistically have in planning for their own health care. The first statement, that consumers will be more responsible for their care, emphasizes a self-care modality with consumers increasingly participating in exercise programs, weight control, seat belt use, decreased alcohol consumption, and smoking cessation programs. These are the consumers who have taken control of their own health and will continue to do so in the future. These consumers will probably have longer life spans and will probably be rewarded for their good health habits by insurers.

As consumers pay more out-of-pocket costs they will choose the services not just by quality, but by cost. For the discharge planner this means that the options and costs will have to be presented to the patient and family. The literature suggests that as patients decide on and pay for services they will also support and work toward the goals of the plan of care. As some consumers will be able to pay for more of the out-of-pocket costs, other consumers will be denied access to services for this reason. Choices for the latter group obviously will be fewer in the future.

The prediction that there will be increased services for the aged will be a welcome change for the consumer as well as for the discharge planner. Although the Little report predicts this change, the financing for such services remains unclear at this time. At the time of this writing there is a great deal of discussion at the federal level regarding insurance for long-term chronic health care.

The shift of care from inpatient to ambulatory settings will clearly have an impact on patients and families in planning for health care. As fewer patients enter the hospital, discharge planning, which most frequently occurs in hospitals, will need to be done in other health care and community settings.

As health care will be increasingly delivered within "managed systems" consumers will be more frequently directed to designated providers of care. The effect of this for consumers is somewhat complex. For the services that are covered within these managed care systems, such as hospitalization, physicians' office visits, laboratory and radiology tests, and home health care, consumers will be directed to providers that have been designated by the insurer. Frequently such decisions are based on cost. Consumers, therefore, will have fewer choices once they choose their insurance plan. In addition to being directed to certain providers of care, consumers will also be directed to receiving care in the least expensive setting; for example, all laboratory and radiology testing will be done in outpatient settings before hospital admission. In this way consumers will be made more aware of the ambulatory and outpatient choices available to them. This is seen as a positive change for consumers, since in the past the inpatient setting was often the only choice. Frequently the difficulty for consumers in managed care systems is choosing the insurance. The complexities of benefits available and costs are difficult for the average health care consumer to analyze.

The absence of the family physician, and the subsequent long-term relationship with that family physician, owing to population mobility and increased physician specialization, leaves the patient and family without that one health care provider who understands the health care needs of both the patient and family. Even though the knowledge of physicians regarding the access to and availability of services within the health care system has been limited, the patient and family in the past have relied on and trusted the physician to steer them through the system. The effect on the patients will be that they will need to rely on other sources and resources to assist them in making their decisions as they move through the health care system.

Consumers in the 1990s will be forced to participate in their own health care decisions because of cost sharing, lack of institutional supports, and the absence of a primary physician.

An important management strategy for client participation in decision making is to involve patients and families as early as possible in the potential choices available to them.

Several health care research studies have concluded that participative decision making enhances goal attainment.[10] When the financial and care issues are significant, or when the decision that will be made means a major change in the patient's or family's life style, the usual course is to have a meeting with the significant players. The meeting can serve many purposes. First, and most important, it can provide the patient and his or her significant family and friends with the potential options facing them in providing long-term care for the patient. Second, very early on it brings the significant family and friends into the decision-making process, which allows that group of people to begin working together on this important issue. As mentioned earlier, consumers will pay more out of pocket, and therefore will become more prudent buyers. Third, as the potential plans are mapped out for the patient and family members, the realistic options begin to come into focus. Fourth, an early meeting allows the family to begin to, if necessary, pull together the financial resources for the patient. This activity frequently takes a while, as patients might own property or homes, and qualifying for the medical assistance programs can take a considerable length of time. Subsequent meetings of the identified significant family and friends with the discharge planner are essential to be sure all are on track in preparing for the patient's movement to the next level of care.

A second strategy for patient participation is to have patients sign their own referrals for health services. Requesting signatures may reinforce their own accountability as they commit to a plan of care. This has been used most efficiently with families in planning for nursing home placement. Financial cooperation is essential to move patients when nursing home beds become available; requesting families to sign letters of agreement assists with placement.

EVALUATION

In order to determine the patient and family satisfaction with the plan of care, an evaluation can be done. This also provides the planner with information on the timeliness and effectiveness of community-based services. Evaluation procedures need to be targeted to clients with complex care needs. To help prevent problems with questionnaires, such as low return rates and the misunderstanding of questions, a structured interview or telephone follow-up is suggested. Exhibit 3-3 lists questions that could be used in a structured telephone interview.

Program evaluation needs to be incorporated at the time of development. Evaluation criteria must be developed to reflect the stated objec-

Exhibit 3-3 Evaluation Tool of Home Care Arrangements

Patient Name:
Phone Number:
Date Discharged:
Date Called:
Agency/Company:
Insurance Source:
Source of Information:

Questions
1. Date service(s) started:

2. Equipment in home; when delivered:

3. Services provided and when started:
   —Nursing
   —Home health aide
   —Physical therapy
   —Occupational therapy
   —Speech therapy
   —Other

4. How are the services you are receiving?

5. Specific problems, if any, that need to be investigated:

tives. The following are some possible measurable objectives that reflect effective program development and management:

- Reduce the average length of stay.
- Decrease the average length of time patients await nursing home placement.
- Increase the number of referrals of patients with high-technology home care needs.
- Decrease the financial loss of a particular DRG.
- Increase the number of referrals to home care agencies, day-care programs, and so on.
- Decrease the number of last-minute delays when patients need to remain hospitalized because plans fall through.

BUDGETING AND COSTS

Your task is to prepare a budget for start-up of a discharge planning program. These are the questions to ask:

- How many staff will I need?
- What is an approximate staffing ratio per number of patients?
- What is an appropriate staffing ratio for hospital size and type?
- How many social workers, nurses, resource workers, and secretarial support staff will I need?
- What will be the mix of professionals to non-professionals?
- How do I justify additional staff in this time of cost containment?

The strategy to be taken with a cost containment program is to estimate the potential savings by implementing a discharge planning program. It is important to remember that the program must be effective to be able to produce these saving measures. It must be well organized, using the appropriate disciplines at the appropriate times; innovative, targeting groups of patients that can receive services in alternative settings; and well managed, staying abreast of the day-to-day management issues as well as the reimbursement and regulatory issues that will affect the discharge planning program. As one sets up the program there are a number of factors that will affect the staffing requirements. The size and complexity of the hospital are issues. For example, if the hospital specializes in cardiac surgery, or if it has a disproportionate number of patients over age 65, or, more important, over age 75, more staff will be needed. The role of the discharge planner is significant. Social workers who are involved in discharge planning may also be responsible for in-depth counseling. Nurses may also have a utilization review role in a hospital setting. These responsibilities will impact on the number of staff needed.

Because each hospital is unique and has different methods of gathering statistics, the manager needs to explore the available information to justify the development of a new department.

In justifying the potential for cost saving, the manager needs to gather some basic data about the organization. This should include the following:

- Average length of stay at hospital compared with national data
- Average length of stay of those over age 65 compared with national statistics
- Average cost per day per patient (what DRGs are revenue losers?)

- Average number of discharges per year
- Percentage of those over age 65 within hospital on any given day
- Percentage of patients placed in nursing homes each month
- Number of patients awaiting nursing home placement each month

Once the manager has obtained this information, it can be used to justify the program's existence as well as to evaluate its impact.

The budget reflects the assumptions and goals of the program. Before the specifics of a budget are outlined, some of the previous assumptions need to be restated. They are (a) that a successful program has a mix of both social workers and nurses; (b) that the discipline responsible for the screening and initial assessment essentially assumes the program management; and (c) that support staff will be used when possible.

The Massachusetts Department of Public Welfare Discharge Planning Regulation has stated that there should be one discharge planner for every 60 patients in the hospital. With adequate secretarial staff, liaison workers, administrative support, and a role limited to discharge planning this ratio can be adequate. When other responsibilities are added, the ratio changes to one planner for every 45 patients.

The discharge planning model in Figure 3-1 supports nursing and social work collaborating within the same department. In this model the continuing care coordinators, seven full-time employees (FTEs), assume the screening function and are primarily responsible for program management. Social work provides counseling and acts as a consultant to the program. This model is based on a ratio of one discharge planner for every 60 patients. It suggests that the discharge planner's time is primarily spent assessing, coordinating, and planning. The implementation of the plan can be shared by the support staff, which includes the liaison workers and the secretaries. The social workers are involved in some discharge planning activities, specifically in the maternal and child health unit, the emergency department, the oncology unit, and the psychiatric unit.

Figure 3-2 is a discharge planning model in which the social work staff provides counseling and primary discharge planning program management. The continuing care coordinators are consultants to the program. The model is based on the ratio of one discharge planner for every 60 patients. It suggests that the discharge planner's time is primarily spent in contact with the patient and family and other disciplines. The support staff, which includes the liaison workers and the secretaries, arranges for many concrete services and acts as liaison with many community-based agencies. The continuing care coordinators are consultants to the social

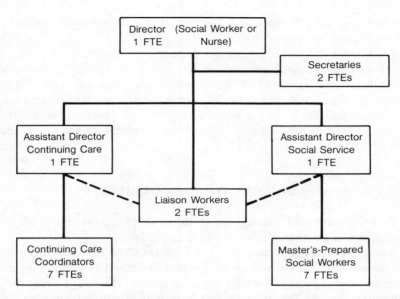

Figure 3-1 Suggested Organizational Model for Discharge Planning Program with Continuing Care Coordinator as Program Manager (for 420-bed community hospital)

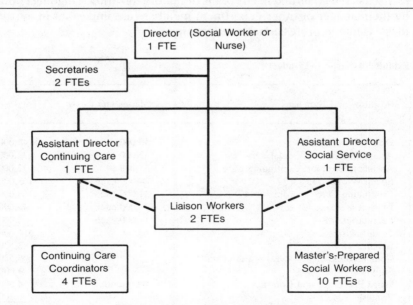

Figure 3-2 Suggested Organizational Model for Discharge Planning Program with Social Worker as Program Manager (for 420-bed community hospital)

workers and are involved in coordinating many complex medical and nursing discharge plans.

The budget in Exhibit 3-4 applies to both proposed models. It suggests a ratio of one discharge planner for every 60 patients. This is adjusted to one planner for every 45 patients when additional responsibilities are added. In the model in Figure 3-2, for example, the social workers do counseling and discharge planning. The number of social workers is therefore increased to ten and continuing care coordinators are decreased to four.

ESTABLISHING LINKAGES TO THE COMMUNITY

To implement and manage an effective discharge planning program, knowledge of community resources is essential.

When establishing a program, the time taken to explore resources in the community will be well spent. Getting to know key contact people in agencies and organizations can expedite future referrals. During the developmental stage the manager needs to gather information about each agency's goals and services. This is also an opportunity for the manager to discuss the goals and needs of his or her organization. Ongoing contacts by the manager or other department members are important in nurturing these valuable professional relationships.

Exhibit 3-4 Suggested Budget

Positions and Expenses	Salaries and Costs	Total
Director	$40,000	$ 40,000
Assistant Director, Social Service	32,000	32,000
Assistant Director, Continuing Care	32,000	32,000
Social Worker Master (7)	24,000 each	168,000
Continuing Care Coordinators (7)	24,000 each	168,000
Liaison Workers (2)	20,000 each	40,000
Secretaries (2)	17,000 each	34,000
Total Salaries		514,000
Benefits 18%		92,520
Combined expenses: salaries and benefits		606,520
Supplies		4,000
Word Processor and Contract	400/month	4,800
Printing		200
Total: Salaries, Benefits, & Costs		$615,520

In setting up a program, designating one or two persons as liaison or resource workers can centralize contacts with community agencies. Once requests or referrals for services or products are made, these workers can be available to iron out the details and confirm arrangements.

Liaison or resource workers can coordinate plans within the discharge planning department with social workers and nurses. Communication and organizational skills, assertiveness, and follow-through are essential for someone in this position. Keep in mind that this person is frequently vying for limited resources and must have the skills to negotiate. He or she is also responsible for coordinating and completing patients' care plans. Credibility is a key factor in future relationships.

The following are some activities that are best accomplished by resource or liaison workers:

- Seeking out and coordinating nursing home placements
- Obtaining equipment and supplies
- Arranging for homemakers (nonprofessional) services
- Arranging for transportation home and to future medical appointments
- Assisting with Medicaid applications

This position is pivotal to the smooth operation of a department. Selecting a person who meets the qualifications already mentioned and who has the communication skills to work responsibly with all the people involved is an important management priority.

When arranging for community services, working closely with patient and families is essential. At this point in the planning it must be assumed that the responsible parties have agreed to the plan. Because availability of resources and financial obligations are frequently involved, patients and families need to be part of ongoing decision making. When arranging for a service that the family will pay for privately, the practice is to provide family members with a list of qualified providers (i.e., homemakers) and let them make their own arrangements.

Once the manager has made the contacts and identified community resources, a central file will make such information available to all staff. Keeping the information current is a task in which all staff must participate. Information to be maintained in the central file includes the following:

- Organization name, address, and phone number
- Contact person
- Purpose

- Organization structure
- Service(s) provided
- Standards, accreditation, or license

The following is a list of organizations and agencies to seek out and establish linkages with:

- Nursing homes
- Home health agencies
- Homemaker or private pay home care agencies
- Area agency on aging
- Personal care homes or residential facilities
- Rehabilitation facilities
- Durable medical equipment or pharmaceutical companies
- Medicaid eligibility offices
- Hospice programs
- Medicaid waiver programs
- State social service departments
- Substance abuse programs
- Legal services for the elderly
- Adult day care
- Adult and child protective services
- Shelters
- American Cancer Society, Multiple Sclerosis Society, American Lung Association, Diabetes Association, etc.

CONCLUSION

The essential considerations in designing a discharge planning program are complex. The manager must be skilled at program development and implementation within the institutional setting. She or he must also become knowledgeable about resources available in the community, to facilitate the necessary linkages between organizations. The intent of this chapter is to outline the problems and issues involved and to present strategies to enable the manager to accomplish this complex task.

NOTES

1. John Feather and Linda Nichols, "Hospital Discharge Planning: The Other Side of Continuity of Care," *Caring,* October 1984, pp. 37–38.

2. Cherie Clausen, "Staff R.N.: A Discharge Planner for Every Patient," *Nursing Management,* November 1984, pp. 58–61.

3. Richard Edwards, "Professionals in Alliance Achieve More Effective Discharge Planning," *Hospitals,* June 1978, pp. 71–72.

4. Paul Reichelt and Jean Newcomb, "Organizational Factors in Discharge Planning," *Journal of Nursing Administration,* December 1980, pp. 36–42.

5. Feather and Nichols, "Hospital Discharge Planning," pp. 37–38.

6. Arthur D. Little, Inc., *The Health Care System in the Mid-1990's,* January 1985, pp. 16–19. Washington, D.C.: The Health Insurance Association of America.

7. N. R. Kleinfield, "When the Boss Becomes the Doctor," *New York Times,* January 5, 1986, Sec. 3, p. 25.

8. The National Association of Home Care, A Report to Congress, "The Attempted Dismantling of the Medicare Home Health Benefit," March 19, 1986, p. 36.

9. Arthur D. Little, Inc., *The Health Care System,* pp. 17–20.

10. Mary Ann Swain and Susan B. Steckel, "Influencing Adherence Among Hypertensives," *Research in Nursing and Health* 4 (1981): 213–22.

REFERENCES

Aaron, Henry J., and Schwartz, William B. *The Painful Prescription.* Washington, D.C.: The Brookings Institution, 1984, pp. 113–34.

Blendon, Robert J. "Health Policy Choices for the 1990s." *Issues in Science and Technology* 2, no. 4 (Summer 1986): 65–73.

Brown, Jean E. "Situational Ethics: An Approach to Resolving Ethical Dilemmas in Discharge Planning." *Discharge Planning Update,* Fall 1984, pp. 7–10.

Califano, Joseph, "A Corporate Rx for America: Managing Runaway Health Costs." *Issues in Science and Technology* 1, no. 3 (Spring 1986): 81–90.

Coulton, Claudia. "Discharge Planning as a Decision-Making Process." *Discharge Planning Update,* Spring 1981, pp. 6–9.

Granatir, Tom. "PRO: Implications for Discharge Planning." *Discharge Planning Update,* Spring 1985 pp. 4–5.

Holland, Thomas P. "Doing Right and Doing Good: Ethical Problems in Practice, An Essay." *Discharge Planning Update,* Winter 1984, pp. 10–14.

Kane, Rosalie A. "Discharge Planning and Multidisciplinary Teamwork: A Cautionary Note." *Discharge Planning Update,* Winter 1982, pp. 9–13.

McKeehan, Kathleen M. *Continuing Care: A Multidisciplinary Approach to Discharge Planning.* St. Louis: C. V. Mosby Co., 1981, pp. 65–94, 119–29.

Chapter 4

Managing the Discharge Planning Program

Charlotte A. Leavitt
Margaret A. Terry
Patricia A. O'Hare

4

For more than a decade nurses and social workers have been responsible for coordinating patients' discharges to ensure continuity of care. They have functioned in a variety of organizational structures with limited administrative sanction and support, few role models, and limited management experience. Engaging other professionals in discharge planning has been the method used to achieve continuity of care.

In 1983 the Prospective Payment System (PPS) entered the acute care picture. Hospitals are now paid for the care they give to Medicare patients based on diagnosis-related groups (DRGs). Discharging patients in a timely manner means a positive bottom line for the institution; however, premature discharges can be a costly liability.

Now, under PPS, effective discharge planning programs are vital to the acute care hospital's survival. Traditional health care delivery systems have responded to this new reimbursement program. Discharge planning managers are challenged to provide the framework for continuing care professionals to carry out the process in this changing environment. The manager's role is to develop and implement systems and activities that will motivate the staff, make appropriate use of resources, and enhance the continuity of care process in the institution.

The business of health care must be understood by discharge planning managers. Health care organizational goals and current reimbursement systems need to be understood and applied to daily work situations. Managers need to be fluent in management theory and techniques to achieve successful results.

MANAGEMENT PROCESS

Management implies systematic operations, behaviors, and interactions with people. Peter Drucker's "management by objectives" was first introduced in the 1950s and continues to be an effective approach. In essence, goals are established and actions are developed to reach certain objectives. Within health care these goal-setting techniques can be used to establish effective discharge planning programs.

Management involves providing services within the mission of the organization. Acute care hospitals are expanding into new markets, such as skilled nursing facilities, home health agencies, walk-in clinics, wellness programs, retail pharmacies, real estate, corporate health care programs, day care (both for adults and children), mobile laboratories, and hotel hospitals. Prospective pricing has meant competition among providers for their share of the market. These new undertakings broaden the hospital's role in providing a more comprehensive approach to consumers in all phases of health care. These new services mean added resources within one's own walls. The discharge planning manager is in a unique position to identify community needs and assist in the evaluation of these new ventures. With hospital corporations interested in the success of these new ventures, discharge planners will be encouraged to use these services. The potential for conflict for the discharge planning manager is evident. With the new importance and stature of discharge planning, managers have opportunities to be involved in the overall direction of the institution. This necessitates that the discharge planning program be in concert with other departments and with the mission of the hospital.

Under PPS, conflicts between the discharge planning program and the financial interests of the institution may arise. Discharge planning managers need to analyze the issues, weighing the financial and legal liabilities, and develop alternatives for resolving them.

When an expeditious discharge is difficult to achieve, the discharge planning manager's responsibility is to clarify the issues for all and assure the patient's safety. Resolution of the discharge planning problems may require further development of resources by the institution.

Managing the discharge planning program in today's health care climate demands clear communications with administration and staff. To achieve continued financial viability, effective and efficient use of acute care resources is required. Timely discharge is an effective method of achieving financial viability. This puts pressure on the discharge planning program. Because of the financial impact, the program manager has to be prepared to shift strategies, take new actions, identify problem areas, and communicate with administration when there are barriers to achieving quality continuity of care plans.

STAFF SELECTION AND PERSONNEL MANAGEMENT

The selection of well-qualified staff who have clinical abilities, knowledge of resources, and knowledge of the health care system assures appropriate planning. Staff development, supervision, and support are top priorities to help staff manage their activities in a role that may present ethical and legal dilemmas. Flexibility, risk taking, rapid action, and creative approaches are techniques required to respond to rapidly changing needs. The constant pressure from the institution to achieve a timely discharge means high stress levels for staff. Communication between staff and manager is necessary to achieve the goal of quality patient care. Managers are challenged to provide the organizational structure and leadership to reduce staff stress.

Before prospective payment most discharge planning programs were clinically oriented, as evidenced by their placement in either the nursing or the social service department. In the June 17, 1986, *Federal Register* the revised Conditions of Participation for hospitals under Medicare were published; they became effective September 15, 1986.[1] These regulations place discharge planning as a component of the Quality Assurance Condition of Participation. How this will affect discharge planning programs remains to be seen. That appropriate discharge is viewed as a measure of quality of care adds credibility to the activities of the continuing care professional.

Discharge planning managers need to be aware that within the organizational structure, the quality assurance program is a new source of support in addition to the clinical areas of nursing and social work. Quality assurance programs are required to be integrated between the medical staff and clinical support services, which gives a broad base of support for discharge planning. However, it also means that the discharge planning manager must be sure that those who are responsible for quality assurance understand what constitutes quality discharge planning.

Discharge planning managers who recognize the shift in emphasis can use it as an additional resource to give credibility to the process and acquire financial resources to assure a quality program. The manager responds by taking advantage of an expanded base of support.

Managers have responsibility for developing systematic operations. Policies, procedures, and guidelines provide the framework for the staff to operate in a consistent manner. In developing policies and procedures the discharge planning manager must incorporate the regulations promulgated by governmental agencies (Health Care Financing Administration [HCFA]) and accrediting bodies (Joint Commission on Accreditation of Hospitals [JCAH]). In addition, managers need to understand the reimbursement guidelines of private third party payers. The dilemma is to establish procedures that address these regulations and guidelines but that remain simple enough to be followed. The following are two examples of policies and procedures that will facilitate the process.

1. *Admission Screening Policy*. The policy states that all admissions will be screened for discharge planning needs. This will meet a requirement of Blue Cross for screening certain diagnoses. It will meet Medicare requirements for discharge planning. It will meet health maintenance organization (HMO) requirements and provide the hospital with additional bargaining power for negotiating contracts with HMOs. The screening process includes documentation of those types of admissions that are screened based on diagnoses, for example, fractured hip, osteomyelitis in a younger person (a good candidate for a home intravenous antibiotic program), a baby who fails to thrive. By monitoring the types of patients who require discharge planning the manager will be able to develop an admission screening policy to meet the institution's needs and more efficiently screen according to each payer's requirements.

2. *Assessment Procedure*. An assessment tool that incorporates such data as demographic, payer, and medical information, functional abilities, specific treatment needs, and laboratory results will mean that the discharge planner has all the necessary information collected for statistical and planning purposes. The insurance information is required to ascertain coverage for posthospital care. The functional limitation is a consideration in recommending ongoing services and referrals to community agencies. Arterial blood gas measurements will determine if there is a need for continuing home oxygen therapy. When negotiating with a long-term care facility the patient's needs are well documented. It is necessary to manage the process efficiently. The collection of demographic data might be a secretarial function, using the hospital computer system. The resources of the various disciplines are needed to gather the information, but the completed assessment will save much time for the discharge planner.

The discharge planning manager must be well informed in order to establish procedures that are efficient and effective and that meet requirements. Changes in regulations mean adaptation of procedures. Local, state, and national continuity of care organizations are good resources to assist the discharge planning manager in staying current. The discharge planning manager develops networks within the institution and community that will keep him or her aware of changes. The discharge planning manager systematically reviews policies and procedures to assure timely revisions.

MANAGEMENT SKILLS

Skills for the effective management of discharge planning programs include:

- establishing measurable objectives,
- implementing actions to achieve objectives,
- evaluating the effectiveness of actions,
- negotiating systems, and
- communicating effectively.

As discharge planning has become more important to the financial viability of hospitals, discharge planners have had increasing responsibility and have moved into management positions. In their day-to-day work with patients they have developed their management skills and need to broaden the application of these skills to program management.

Objectives should be clearly stated, measurable, based on accepted practice, and achievable. As external forces change, the objectives will need to be revised. Two examples of objectives: (1) the discharge planning program will include all areas of the institution and (2) the discharge planning process will begin on admission.

Initially, discharge planning was limited to the medical-surgical units. As can be seen by objective (1), discharge planning has now expanded to include all areas. Implementation of a day surgery program added that unit to the discharge planning program. The availability of home ventilator care means that discharge planning is taking place even in the intensive care unit. Objective (2) needs to be revised to include preadmission discharge planning for elective surgical admissions, in the climate of prospective payment.

Actions that the discharge planning manager might implement to achieve these objectives are based on established practice, clinical knowledge, and the effective use of resources, and include the following:

- Posting the names of the assigned staff members for each unit
- Developing a screening procedure and tool for initial assessment of discharge planning needs
- Implementing a similar screening process with the physician's office staff for preadmission elective surgery and same-day surgery

Evaluating how well the actions achieve the objectives is important. If it becomes evident that not all admissions are being screened, then it is necessary to review the procedure. In reviewing the procedure a determination can be made as to whether the problem is with the procedure or with the personnel. The manager would reassign staff or request funding for additional staff if indicated.

Setting objectives, implementing actions, and evaluating effectiveness will provide structure and consistency for the staff and demonstrate the direction of the program.

For the program to be effective and to be integrated into the overall institution, the discharge planning manager must negotiate systems. To negotiate the systems within the institution requires an understanding of the organizational structure. An important element in continuity of care is obtaining physician's orders for home care. Having physicians complete orders for care is a perennial problem. Knowledge of the organizational structure helps to identify whether an issue should be addressed through committees, such as utilization management or patient care evaluation, or through the chief of service at department meetings.

The integration of hospital departments and committees with the medical staff can affect the implementation and management of the discharge planning program. Patient teaching may be identified as a problem in patients being prepared for discharge. Depending on how nursing is organized, this might be handled either through the patient education committee or through working with specific clinicians who are responsible for patient teaching.

Discharge planning managers also need to negotiate systems outside the institution. The manager might work with a frequently used community agency to develop procedures that will expedite the process of patient referral. It is necessary to assess the problem from the perspective of the receiving agency as well as from the perspective of the referring institution to find procedures that will be beneficial to both.

The community resources that are involved with the continuing care of the patient also have complex organizational structures that the manager must understand in order to work efficiently and effectively with them. A classic example is the state Medicaid program. Vital to the provision of continuing care for patients is the prior approval for services from Medicaid. Identification of the appropriate area and people to contact for approval requires well-developed formal and informal communication systems.

The discharge planning manager must communicate effectively. The direction that the department takes in the overall organization of the institution depends on the manager's ability to influence others and articulate the importance of the department. The effectiveness of the program is enhanced by the manager's relationships with community resources and the communication of the institution's perspective on discharge planning. When DRGs were implemented in Massachusetts, there already was much public concern regarding inappropriate or premature discharges. A local senior center responded by setting up a program to help senior citizens who were prematurely discharged. Through a close working relationship with the senior center the discharge planning manager was able to explain the discharge planning process to them. A program was held to address the issue, and the communication helped the senior citizens and the center's staff develop programs to work more closely with the hospital.

Personal skills essential to effective management of the discharge planning program include leadership and communication. From these skills, experience, and the manager's placement within the organizational structure can come power and authority.

Leadership is a set of actions that influence members of the group to move toward goal setting and goal attainment.[2] In order to influence, the leader must possess a strong vision of the goal and have the ability to make that goal meaningful to the members of the group.

Participatory management is an accepted management practice in health care. Through this practice group members are involved in the process. This style of management provides for meaningful involvement of the employees, which helps in implementing decisions. What usually happens in this practice is that the leader uses different styles to manage different situations. The discharge planning manager will need to be autocratic in requiring that documentation of the discharge plan be completed on every patient. This approach is necessary from a risk management standpoint because complete documentation is essential. On the other hand the scheduling of the individual worker's time can be flexible, meeting caseload requirements but also giving the worker some discretion within broad parameters set by the manager to assure overall department coverage.

The discharge planning manager is uniquely challenged to coordinate a program that depends on others who are not directly responsible to him or her. The actions of people in a variety of departments within the institution and of people employed in agencies outside the institution impact greatly on the effectiveness of the discharge planning program. The success of the program in part depends on the power and influence of the manager and staff. Power is defined in different ways, but in general it means one's ability or capacity to influence others.

The discharge planning manager's power comes from a variety of sources. In working with a community agency the manager's power is present because the discharge planning program is a major source of referrals for the community agency. Therefore, if the agency does not respond as expected, referrals will be diverted to another resource.

Expertise is a form of power. The manager who possesses knowledge of the regulatory process will gain credibility with agencies payed by third party reimbursement. A strong clinical base will gain the respect of physicians and other clinicians, thereby gaining support for the activities of the discharge planning program.

Informal sources of power are also important to develop. Alliances and coalitions help to develop a power base and the credibility necessary to make the program effective.

Authority, although related to power, is more specific. It is legitimate power based on the manager's position and role within the organizational structure of the institution. The position as department head will afford the discharge planning manager power comparable to that of other department heads. For program effectiveness, administration must recognize its value and the manager must have the authority to implement the program.

Discharge planning for continuity of care is still a new specialty area in health care. Many institutions are only beginning to understand its value; acute care institutions are more developed, and now nursing homes, HMOs, home health agencies, and other settings are developing programs. The manager must secure the authority needed to conduct an effective program. The new manager will experience frustration if the necessary authority hasn't been attained within the organizational structure.

Regulations legitimize and mandate the manager's position and authority in the organization. Discharge planning is a Condition of Participation for hospitals in the Medicare program. Discharge planning is incorporated in the JCAH standards for nursing and social work. It is expected that more specific standards for discharge planning will be developed. However, it is still important for the manager to develop a broad power base and to position the department within the organizational structure where it is most effective. In today's turbulent health care environment the manager must be aware of change and act as necessary. Discharge planning is now viewed as a quality assurance activity and has important implications for risk management. Both of these activities provide the manager with additional power and authority.

The discharge planning manager and staff motivate others to actively participate in the discharge planning process. Basic motivators are achievement, self-esteem, positive reinforcement, challenge, clear communication, and respect. It is necessary to have systems in place that provide a mechanism for feedback to all who are part of the discharge planning process. For example, reports received from community resources such as home health agencies or equipment companies would be shared with the primary nurse in the institutional setting as well as with the physician. The nurse will be able to assess whether or not the assessment and plan were appropriate as well as receive information regarding the patient's progress. Team meetings, follow-up reports, and quality assurance studies are examples of systems that will help to motivate people to participate in the discharge planning process (see Figure 4-1).

The need to effect change is a frequent challenge to the manager. To effect change it is necessary to analyze the system, develop the process, implement the plans, and, finally, stabilize the change. The analysis of the system includes:

- identifying positive and negative factors of the problem,
- determining alternatives,

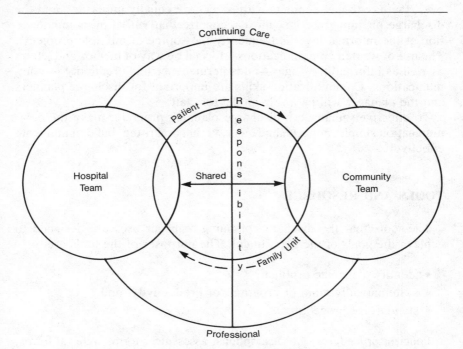

Figure 4-1 Bridging the Gap. *Source:* Charlotte A. Leavitt.

- exploring the ramifications of the alternatives,
- assessing resources,
- recognizing the phases of change, and
- choosing the techniques to be implemented.

In effecting change the manager needs to develop techniques that will reinforce and build on the positive or driving forces and reduce the negative or restraining forces. The discharge planning manager would do well to remember that "if you want to bring about change you have to do it in steps."[3]

The skill that ranks number one for successful management of the discharge planning program is communication. Communication with staff is necessary to impart the goals, concepts, and vision of the program. Communication with community agencies is essential for the development of quality discharge plans.

Communication means oral and written, formal and informal. The discharge planning manager may want to use departmental, interdepartmental, and interagency meetings to effect formal oral communication. However, the day-to-day contacts with others are equally important, and the discharge planning manager must recognize that verbal miscommunication at the informal level is frequently the source of multiple problems. The use of written communications—formal by way of memos and letters as well as informal messages—adds permanence and credibility to communications. Communication skills are important for discharge planners and the manager will be a role model for staff.

To effectively manage a discharge planning program, make the communication simple, concise, and clear, verbal or written, but communicate effectively.

TOOLS AND RESOURCES

The tools that the discharge planning manager uses are designed to achieve the goals of the department. The purposes of the tools are to:

- identify a specific problem,
- systematically monitor programs or productivity, and
- standardize procedures.

Policies, procedures, job descriptions, assessment forms, referral forms, agency evaluation tools, statistical forms, and follow-up forms are examples of tools to assist in the management of the program. Those who will be using the tools need to participate in their development.

Within the institution there is a need for careful understanding of what resources are available to achieve new goals for the discharge planning program. The discharge planning manager would be involved in the more formal political process of initiating and supporting legislative activities that enhance continuity of care. This activity is best carried out through state and national associations for continuity of care.

The resources available to assist the manager include the literature and local, state, and national organizations for continuity of care. Local and state organizations offer the opportunity for sharing knowledge and providing peer support. The emphasis is on local resources, regulations, and legislative impact. The American Association for Continuity of Care (AACC) is a national organization offering programs, the opportunity for sharing ideas, and expertise. The National Association of Social Workers and the American Hospital Association frequently sponsor workshops and programs on discharge planning. Participation in organizations is a way to affect the development of health care policy.

INTERDISCIPLINARY PERSPECTIVE

To be effective, continuity of care must be a shared responsibility of all disciplines involved with patient care. The manager must develop systems within the institution that engage all of the professional disciplines in the program. This may be done by a discharge planning committee composed of representatives who are key people in their departments or disciplines. It may be achieved by developing relationships with individual departments or through administrative directive. In the DRG climate the impetus for discharge planning is fiscally driven. A combination of approaches is the usual route that is necessary. Turf issues are inherent, and the discharge planning manager must be prepared to deal with them and to assist staff in their day-to-day activities when turf issues interfere.

Managers need to assess their own situations to identify the strategy that will yield the most effective results. It is also important for the manager to realize that the strategy used may have to be altered as the institution's climate changes. The discharge planning manager must clearly identify the fiscal benefits to a proactive program and, when the timing is right, emphasize these fiscal benefits. The quality of patient care is most important to emphasize.

The unique challenge to each member of the discharge planning staff is to effectively coordinate each discipline's approach, as shown in Figure

4-2. This aspect of the discharge planning process means that the program manager:

- selects staff with excellent interpersonal skills,
- provides staff development in communication skills,
- develops an environment within the institution that allows staff to coordinate effectively, and
- recognizes the high potential for staff burnout.

INTERAGENCY PERSPECTIVE

The discharge planning program must relate to and usually depends on other agencies or facilities for the successful implementation of plans. Figure 4-3 shows relationships with other agencies, and Figure 4-1 depicts

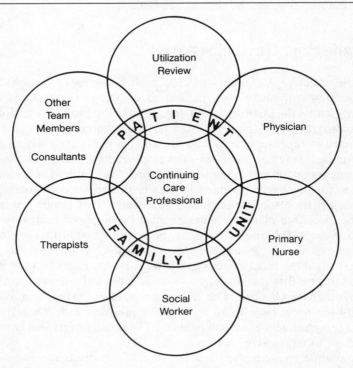

Figure 4-2 Hospital Coordination. *Source:* Charlotte A. Leavitt.

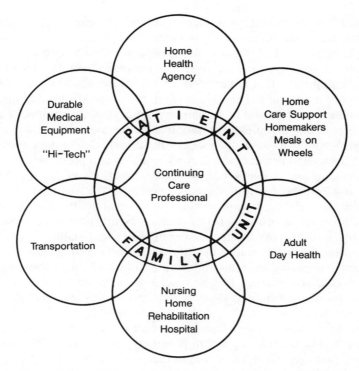

Figure 4-3 Community Coordination. *Source:* Charlotte A. Leavitt.

the role of the continuing care program in bridging the gap from one setting to another. This presents a second challenging problem for the manager.

The discharge planning manager needs to continually assess community organizations to assure standards of care and service availability. Through these contacts both community agency and institution can work collaboratively to effect change.

These activities can be achieved through:

- formal, regularly scheduled administrative meetings,
- joint staff development programs,
- joint clinical case conferences, and
- joint quality assurance studies.

Conflicts can occur when two organizations with different goals work together, but systems can be developed to lessen such conflicts. The role of HMO liaison nurses, insurance personnel, hospice staff, home care professionals, and other outside personnel in the acute care setting is an example of a new phenomenon. All outside people who come to the institution bring their own perspective. The hospice nurse has a supportive, palliative approach that is very different from the active treatment interventions of acute care. The liaison personnel from HMOs and insurance companies are interested in minimizing the cost of institutional care and moving patients as quickly as possible to the next level of care. The manager's role is to develop systems that clearly define the expectations of each, as well as protect patient confidentiality and preserve the integrity of the institution. Table 4-1 shows some functions of an HMO liaison nurse and a hospital continuing care nurse.

In the current health care environment, community agencies and facilities are even more important. Resources must be developed in the community to provide the increasing intensity and skilled level of care. The manager has a key role in identifying the services that patients require and then in engaging agencies and facilities in developing services to meet those needs. A challenge for the discharge planning manager is the involvement, interaction, and dependency on agencies and facilities outside the institution.

Many institutions are developing their own home health agencies, skilled nursing facilities, adult day health programs, and so forth. The discharge planning manager plays a key role in this process. Whether it be a newly established venture, a joint venture, or a contractual arrangement to assure availability of resources, the manager should be an integral part of

Table 4-1 Functions of HMO Liaison Nurse and Continuing Care Nurse

HMO Liaison Nurse	Continuing Care Nurse
Benefits interpretation	Admission screening
Liaison with	Coordination within hospital
patient and plan physician	Assess for anticipated discharge plan
physician and continuing care nurse	Develop discharge plan, using HMO providers
hospital and community providers	Evaluation of provider agencies
Reinforce discharge plan	Documentation of discharge planning process
Continuity from plan to hospital	in medical record
Individual care management	
Faciltate nursing home transfers	
Approve discharge plan for payment	

Source: Charlotte A. Leavitt.

the development and operation. The decisions that are made by the manager depend on careful analysis of interagency relationships.

COMPETITION

Competition among community agencies for market shares places stressful demands on the discharge planning program. Discharge planning managers evaluate providers, meet with account representatives, and develop systems to offer choices to patients. The actions taken have to be in concert with the philosophy of the institution.

In addition, HMOs and insurance companies are identifying preferred providers. The discharge planning manager has to alter the program to incorporate these special programs. The decisions made by the manager depend on the policy of the institution and terms negotiated with the HMO or insurance company. The discharge planning staff may be entirely responsible for planning for ongoing care or may be responsible for integrating personnel from the payers of care into the institutional setting. The manager carefully analyzes the implications of the system implemented to assure that it is one that will meet the standards, objectives, and philosophy of the program. The manager provides input to administration when contracts are being negotiated.

Likewise, as hospitals recognize the need for relationships with community providers to facilitate timely posthospital services, the discharge planning program manager must be part of the process. The manager has current information about community organizations and resources and is responsible to assist administration in determining those that are best able to meet the institution's needs. The discharge planning department is an important link to the community. The manager with access to top administration enhances organizational decision making.

SERVICE DELIVERY

Discharge planning programs may differ greatly. The manager has important decisions to make about how the program functions within the institution. Some discharge planning programs provide direct service, whereas others provide consultation only.

In practice, the discharge planning department usually functions in different ways, depending on the types of cases and the skills of primary caregivers. It is the role of the discharge planning manager to assess the needs of the institution and plan the program to meet these needs. The decisions made will determine staffing patterns, the skills of staff, the kind of staff development required, and the roles of discharge planning professionals. The manager reassesses on a regular basis as institutional changes occur. If several new nurses start on a unit, that unit will require more assistance from discharge planners while the new staff are developing their skills. Flexibility in managing the program will allow more cost-effective discharge planning.

REIMBURSABLE SERVICES

Regulations and reimbursement, which limit choices for patients, impact on the operation of the discharge planning program. Patients and families have limited knowledge of these complex issues. A common response when exploring payment sources for services is "Mother has Medicare, so everything is taken care of." Patients and families are not aware of Medicare regulations for home care, which limit services to patients who are "homebound" and require "skilled care on an intermittent basis." Many patients require personal care with no intermittent skilled care. Others could be discharged home with twice-a-day dressing changes, which means that they may exceed the criteria for intermittent care. Medicare's coverage for home health care is very limited in meeting the long-term care needs of the elderly. Likewise, the majority of patients requiring nursing home care do not meet Medicare's criteria for nursing home care.

Similarly those patients who may qualify for Medicaid need to understand the eligibility requirements and benefits. Even those patients who have private insurance are frequently unaware of the procedure for making a claim or what their policy covers. They may be unaware of preferred providers or the preapprovals necessary for care. The discharge planning manager should assess and develop creative ways of educating patients and families to deal with these issues. Some suggestions are:

- group educational programs,
- video educational programs,
- brochures, and
- written instructions to assist with adherence.

Informing patients and families of the service available and potential costs is difficult because of the complexity of the system and the lack of knowledge of the consumer.

PATIENT ADVOCACY

Discharge planning personnel frequently find themselves in conflict as they advocate for patients and are working to prevent financial loss for the institution. Under the DRGs the institutional goal of early discharge may be in conflict with patient needs. The discharge planners' advocacy for patients is based on objective data. In working with community resources the discharge planner advocates for patients to secure services regardless of payment sources.

Discharge planning professionals can advocate for patients through their local, state, and national organizations. Program managers have the data to identify gaps in services, reimbursement problems, inappropriate resources, and other concerns in offering quality continuity of care. Through their organizations, data can be collected and presented to appropriate sources, such as Nursing Home Ombudsmen, Elder Legal Services, and Area Agencies on Aging. The manager advocates for patients through active involvement in such community organizations as the Multiple Sclerosis Society, the American Cancer Society, the American Lung Association, and the Diabetes Association.

STATISTICS

For the discharge planning manager, statistics are a valuable tool. The availability of accurate and applicable data is crucial for the viability of the program. Program statistics serve many purposes. The type of information collected depends on how it will be used. This means determining what is pertinent in each setting. The following are a few suggestions for using discharge planning data:

- Implementing quality assurance
- Managing productivity
- Planning cost accounting
- Budgeting
- Identifying gaps in service
- Establishing credibility with community organizations
- Affecting change
- Projecting future trends
- Developing programs

The type of data collected may change as the program evolves.

Table 4-2 Use of Data

Data	Application
Referral source Discipline Nursing unit	Quality assurance Staff development Staffing patterns Cost accounting
Number of home care referrals	Quality assurance Projecting trends Gaps in service
Nursing home placements	Future planning
Required services in the home	Gaps in service Future planning
Patient origin	Gaps in service Affecting change
Patients waiting for nursing home placement	Financial impact Gaps in service Future planning
Payer source	Affecting change Gaps in service
Age	Trends Future planning
Referrals managed by individual staff	Productivity Staffing patterns Budgeting

Source: Charlotte A. Leavitt.

Table 4-2 shows types of data collected and their uses. In many cases there are multiple applications, and depending on individual settings, the data may be used in different ways.

Statistics for quality assurance will be covered in more detail in the section on quality assurance. Frequently data collected for other reasons will reveal problems of quality and identify a need for more detailed study.

Productivity is increasingly important as health care facilities struggle with cost containment. To evaluate productivity, data must be collected and analyzed. The discharge planning program's productivity is the basis for changes in staffing patterns. The change may be in staff assignment, documenting the need for additional staff or, in rare cases, the need to cut back. The difficulty encountered by discharge planning managers is finding an accurate unit of measurement. The review of statistics in relation to individual staff assignments will give an indication of productivity; however, the number of referrals completed does not take into consideration the work involved with each one. To accurately measure the time spent on each case is burdensome for staff, probably not consistently accurate, and certainly not cost-effective. By establishing the time required for the various activities involved in discharge planning, a system can be developed that classifies the work. The acuity classification criteria are helpful in assigning discharge planning costs to specific patient care units for cost accounting and for monitoring staff productivity. Such a system is described by Patricia Hanson of Health Care Management Services in her handbook. A similar system to identify needed staffing changes is outlined in Table 4-3.

A time study is often necessary. Staff need to be part of the planning and development of a classification system to assure cooperation and accuracy. Once the system has been established, the discharge planning manager has a tool to manage productivity. Factors other than caseload must be considered in measuring productivity. They include regularly scheduled activities (staff meetings), vacation time, sick time, census of the institution, and seasonal variation.

The discharge planning program manager can monitor the staff's productivity on a weekly or monthly basis. The data system should be established based on the needs of the department and the institution.

Cost accounting has become important as hospitals struggle to deliver cost-effective care under PPS. Discharge planning programs are generally not revenue producing, and the service provided needs to be accounted for in a different way. Some discharge planning programs are developing revenue-producing programs. One such example is a program for people in the community who need assistance in assessing needs, exploring alternatives, accessing services, understanding reimbursement, and coordinating services. It is called SEARCH and is marketed to physicians' offices, senior citizens' groups, and community organizations. Although a small part of the overall program, it is a response to requests from outside the hospital and has met the needs of clients. Plus, it has generated revenue for the department.

Finally, the challenge for every discharge planning manager is to identify areas of cost saving to the institution based on the effectiveness of the department's work. If effective discharge planning results in early discharge of patients, these days are revenue for the institution. Discharge planning managers should be aware of days saved and use these data for justification with administration.

Table 4-3 Acuity Classification Criteria

Classification I	*15 minutes or less*

1. Patients identified for continuing care management who, after review by continuing care nurse, require no further assessment or intervention by continuing care
2. Screening only
3. Routine maternal child health referrals

Classification II	*15 minutes to 1 hour*

1. Patients identified for continuing care management whose assessment and intervention are limited to chart review
   1 patient/family interview
   1 contact with other professional
   1 referral call
2. Return to nursing home same level within 10 days and requires no more than two phone calls to nursing home
3. Nursing home patients who expire within 48 hours of admission
4. Early maternity discharge program

Classification III	*1–3 hours*

1. Uncomplicated referrals for HMO patients
2. Patients who require assessment and intervention with:
   2–4 patient/family contacts
     two disciplines in addition to physician
     involvement in case with 2–4
     professional consultations
   2–4 calls to referral agencies
3. Nursing home patients who return to same facility with one of the following:
   a. same level with extension no more than two phone calls
   b. level change within 10 days
   c. same level with 10 days and more than two phone calls

Classification IV	*3–5 hours*

1. Patients requiring assessment and intervention involving:
   5–8 patient/family contacts
   5–8 intrahospital professional coordination contacts
2. New nursing home placement facility contacts and application forms—no more than two

continues

Table 4-3 continued

Classification IV	3–5 hours

3. Return to same nursing home with level change and in excess of 10 days
4. Nursing home patients who expire in excess of 10 days

Classification V*	5 hours +

1. Ventilator patients
2. Patients hospitalized in excess of 2 months
3. Patients discharged home on TPN/IV/enteral feedings
4. Insurance coverage confirmation required
5. Any patient who requires individual case management through the insurance provider
6. Patients who require coordination of three or more community service providers
7. New nursing home placement within three or more facility contacts or application forms

*Please estimate actual time involved.
Source: Charlotte A. Leavitt.

In preparing a budget for the discharge planning program, data regarding change in volume, intensity, and type of service are essential for budgetary preparation (see section on budgeting).

An example of the use of statistics for affecting change occurred in Massachusetts in 1984–85. Representatives of four social work and continuing care organizations formed the Coalition for Cost Effective Discharge Planning.[4] They gathered statistics from continuing care professionals across the state and presented them to the Case Management and Screening Program (CMSP) of Medicaid. Their work, documented by accurate data, changed the focus of the Medicaid program. Hospitals were given the option of being delegated to determine levels of care, thus leaving CMSP personnel more available for community activities.

Statistics regarding durable medical equipment (DME) needs and actual resources used are valuable when meeting with company representatives in the current competitive climate. At times DME company representatives present information that indicates a greater need than actually exists. Statistics are helpful in examining the actual need for these products. Statistics allow the manager to discuss realistic referral levels and patient equipment needs. The data may show a change in the age of people served or in the number who require nursing home care or home intravenous antibiotics. The trends shown by statistics impact on future planning.

How statistics will be compiled, stored, and analyzed is a question that the discharge planning manager must answer. Should the process be computerized? Bruce Pinchbeck, in his presentation at the 1985 Conference of the American Association for Continuity of Care on "Computers in Discharge Planning Management—The Basics," addressed this question. He gives the following advantages of computerizing:

- Large amounts of data are easily stored.
- The computer can search and return data quickly.
- The data can be arranged in various forms, sorted and analyzed.
- It is usually easy to enter data.

The following are limitations of the computer:

- There is not unlimited storage.
- Computers cannot differentiate accurate from inaccurate information.

Those responsible must be accurate, motivated, and eager.[5] Computerizing the data from the discharge planning program and sharing these data with administration will increase the power base for discharge planning within the organization.

In evaluating the cost of computerizing the data, it is necessary to compare the cost of doing it manually with the cost of the computer itself, as well as with the cost of inputting data and retrieving information from the computer. Whether to use a personal computer or the hospital mainframe is an important decision. Factors to be considered include the resources available in the institution and the value of being able to access data that originate in other departments, such as medical records, fiscal services, and quality assurance.

Statistics are extremely important in the management of the program. They provide the documentation for decision making regarding cost-effective quality service. Computerizing the data enhances the process of using statistics.

DETERMINING REASONABLE CASELOADS

How to determine a reasonable caseload is a question that plagues every discharge planning manager. Factors involved in caseload determination include age, diagnosis(es), socioeconomic issues, psychosocial issues, program organization, utilization of support personnel, and availability of community resources.

The discharge planner whose assignment is on a neurological unit may have more complex cases than someone on a gynecology unit. Determining a reasonable caseload can be better evaluated by developing a system of assigning values to tasks required. Patients who require the following care are more involved; therefore, the discharge planner's work is more involved:

• Multiple services
• Multiple agencies
• Minimal family supports
• Conflict between patient and family or within family regarding the patient's care
• Limited community resources
• Limited financial coverage
• Individual case management availability
• Physician involvement problematic

These items are all part of a patient classification system, and if the caseload is monitored by classifying patients, patterns will be seen. The classifications are then translated into time. Thus the average number of patients that can be managed by the individual discharge planner can be determined (refer to Table 4-3). The criteria developed will be standardized and easily monitored. To determine what is reasonable to expect workers to manage, staff should be involved in identifying what is appropriate. They should also be involved in ongoing monitoring to make necessary changes. Staff members need to feel that they are carrying equivalent caseloads. The data collected by using an acuity classification criteria system are helpful to the manager in documenting that staff caseloads are equal.

The staff's interest area and special expertise are necessary considerations in estimating each worker's productivity. Arbitrary assignment of numbers of cases omits these two important considerations. The manager's role is to know the staff and make assignments that will enhance productivity.

As discussed in Chapter 3, in 1982 the Massachusetts Department of Public Welfare Discharge Planning Regulations stated that there should be one discharge planner for every 60 patients in the acute care setting. This sparked much controversy for the following reasons:

- Type of patient mix
- Age
- Socioeconomic factors
- Psychosocial factors
- Involvement of primary nurse in discharge planning
- Community resources

The two organizational models shown in Chapter 3 suggest the applicability of this formula. When the support staff is removed, the ratio decreases significantly. The type of discharge planning program an institution has impacts on the ratio of patients to discharge planners that is required at that institution.

As acute care hospitals broaden their discharge planning programs to include preadmission planning, seven-days-a-week coverage, and 24-hour emergency department coverage, the ability to determine appropriate caseloads becomes even more complicated. The role of the manager is to develop a system to monitor staff activities to see that the patients who require discharge planning for continuity of care are serviced, and that the staff's work assignments are appropriate for the time worked.

To manage effectively, productivity is the goal. The development of a system, based on agreed criteria, will help the process. It may be called acuity classification, service intensity, or some other descriptive term. It will provide documentation for administration of the work of discharge planning. The discharge planning manager must realize that the discharge planning program is competing with all other areas for a piece of the institution's resources, and that the resources will be allocated to those who can show what the results will be. By correlating staffing needs with statistics regarding delayed discharges that result in financial loss to the institution, the case is made for administrative support.

A factor that impacts heavily on the work load of the discharge planner is the individual case management approach, which many health care insurers are implementing in an effort to cut costs. The key to this approach is that the patient's care will be provided in the least costly setting. Discharge planners are being asked to do comparative cost analysis between the acute care institution and the alternative setting, for example, home care or skilled nursing facility. The results certainly are that options are thoroughly explored, the insurance company makes a commitment to pay, and the patient receives the care. However, one or two of these cases impact heavily on the staff's work load. This type of activity illustrates the need to monitor the changing work load for the discharge plan-

Exhibit 4-1 Weekly Productivity Summary/Date:

Nurse	1	2	3	4	5	TOTALS
Classification I						
Classification II						
Classification III						
Classification IV						
Classification V						
Other Activities In-hospital Out-of-hospital Comments						

Source: Charlotte A. Leavitt.

ning program, thereby being able to adapt to changing pressures (see Table 4-3 and Exhibit 4-1).

Data available allow the manager to demonstrate to administration the changes that are occurring. The question for the manager is whether or not the resources involved are yielding sufficient results to continue the input. Innovative and creative activities will reap benefits in increased patient satisfaction as well as improved staff morale and productivity.

BUDGETING

Budgeting is difficult for any manager, but it is a most important part of his or her role. The budget sets the direction for the department to move forward. It projects what it will cost to provide the services of the discharge planning program. It depends on the objectives of the department, is validated by the statistics, and is anticipatory.

When preparing the budget the manager must plan for new programs, consider what is happening with case mix, and project the expected cost of providing services. An example of a new service might be the development of a videocassette training program for primary nurses. It would be necessary to budget for staff time as well as the cost of materials.

The objectives are the guidelines for the kinds of activities that are needed to reach the goals. Careful analysis of the activities will allow the manager to estimate their cost. Things to be included in the budget are staffing patterns (professional and clerical), support, staff education, seminars/travel, supplies (forms, stationery, etc.), marketing, and equipment, such as computer software.

The statistics previously discussed are the documentation required for budget preparation. The budget is a vital component in the management of the discharge planning program. It is important to prepare it carefully based on solid data. Guidance in the budgeting process can be obtained from fiscal services. Because the discharge planning program is not usually revenue producing, the program's value must be justified in other ways. Such justification might include days saved by planning effectively, discharging patients with adequate service, and preventing costly readmissions. Another justification would include identifying problem DRGs to decrease revenue losses, thus demonstrating the role of discharge planning.

QUALITY ASSURANCE

Quality assurance (QA) is a major concern in today's health care environment. Since JCAH was established in 1951, it has had an emphasis on quality of care. The standards

- emphasize a coordinated hospitalwide program;
- allow flexibility in methods of problem identification, assessment, and resolution;
- emphasize a need to focus on activities that have a significant impact on patient care;
- focus on areas in which problem resolution can be demonstrated;
- encourage use of multiple data sources to identify problems; and
- discourage the use of quality assurance studies only for the purpose of documenting high-quality care.

Table 4-4 Quality Assurance Monitors

Standard	Monitor	Exceptions
1. All patients should receive discharge planning.	1. Screen all patients within first working day.	1. Pregnancy
2. Discharge planning documented in medical record.	2. a. Discharge planning note in record *or* b. Primary nurse's note specifies discharge plan.	2. None
3. Discharge planning includes patient and family involvement.	3. Significant other identified in discharge planning note.	3. No family
4. Discharge planning is multidisciplinary.	4. Transfer information includes a. physician's signed order, b. nursing care plan, c. therapist plan, and d. social worker plan.	4. a. None b. None c. Not required d. Not required

Source: Charlotte A. Leavitt.

PPS has added a new concern for quality assurance. To remain financially viable under PPS, there is the incentive to restrict the use of inpatient resources, thereby increasing the risk of reduced quality. The 1986 scope of work for Peer Review Organizations (PROs) emphasized quality. PROs are monitoring all readmissions within specified times for evidence of inappropriate discharge.

Discharge planning is considered a component of quality assurance, as evidenced by the Revised Conditions of Participation for Medicare and Medicaid that became effective September 15, 1986. Under this Condition of Participation, discharge planning is part of quality assurance. Increased credibility is given to discharge planning by this regulation. As a result, accountability and careful monitoring of the discharge planning process increases.

What is quality assurance? It is a systematic evaluation to monitor care. How is the evaluation accomplished? Step one is to identify the standard that is expected to be met. The manager is responsible for establishing standards, and may wish to look to AACC for help. The AACC Task Force on Standards, with membership approval, has recently developed discharge planning standards. (See Chapter 5 for the AACC Standards.)

The establishment of monitors is the current emphasis of JCAH. Table 4-4 shows how monitors to measure certain standards are established.

Step two is problem identification. Some methods of identifying problems include staff conferences, systematic review of medical records and patient care referral forms, investigation of patient complaints, information received from other professionals, and follow-up questionnaires or interviews.

Step three includes studies of specific identified problems to establish how the problems can be resolved.

Step four is the remedial action taken.

Step five is additional study to ascertain if the remedial action is effective.

Frequently one area of study will lead to other areas to explore. For example, several staff members were concerned that patients were not being seen by the home health agency when requested. It was decided to study this jointly with the home health agency that receives 64 percent of the hospital's referrals. A sample for one month was studied. The results showed that 12 percent were not seen when requested. The staff had felt that the standard was 100 percent. Subsequent investigation of the 12 percent showed that there was reasonable justification for the variance. While gathering the data for this study it was discovered that many referrals did not state when the first visit should occur. The staff agreed that the acceptable standard was that the date of the first visit should be stated. Another study will be done to determine the extent of the problem. Involving the staffs from both agencies in this study provided a setting for education and collaboration to improve care.

An example of systematic monitoring is a program of follow-up telephone contacts. A questionnaire developed by the continuing care staff is used by a volunteer who calls patients within two weeks of discharge. The volunteer asks a series of questions related to the following:

- Information about their involvement with the continuing care nurse before discharge
- Actual services they have received at home
- Their perception of the adequacy of the services to meet their needs
- Their perception of the appropriateness of their discharge

This approach has identified problems that can be further studied, has provided information regarding community resources, and has been a good public relations tool.

Designing a quality assurance program for discharge planning involves agencies and facilities outside the institution. Joint activities are ideal but are not easily negotiated. If all parties can realize that they share the responsibility for continuity of care for patients, then joint activities for quality assurance are reasonable.

Table 4-5 Quality Assurance Activites

Quality Assurance Activity	*Discharge Planning Process*
Licensing	Staff qualifications
Study of first contact	Screening for high-risk needs
	Timeliness of discharge
	planning process
Retrospective chart review	Documentation
Concurrent review of interagency	Coordination
referral form	Accuracy of transfer information
Patient questionnaire	Patient and family teaching
	Community resources
	Appropriateness of discharge
Source: Charlotte A. Leavitt.	

By scheduling staff meetings for the purpose of quality assurance, staff will become more aware of and involved with the process. Documentation is a perennial problem for health care professionals, and discharge planning staff members are no exception. The staff complained that they couldn't find required information when covering for one another. A study was designed, and a random sample of records of discharged patients was reviewed. The staff had predetermined the standard for documentation. The results of the study indicated that there was inadequate documentation. The remedial action was to redesign the form used for documentation to provide consistency. A follow-up study done several months later revealed 100 percent compliance. The staff's involvement in this study was educational.

Table 4-5 suggests quality assurance activities and the part of the discharge planning process that is studied. Those items that involved intra-agency activities will be studied through internal systems. Items that are interagency require cooperation and a sense of shared responsibility.

The need for an institutionwide perspective for quality assurance is important for the manager to consider in planning quality assurance activities. The idea of studies and activities done jointly with other departments is very natural for discharge planners because of the interaction with others in attaining the goal of quality care. An example of a joint study with nursing was to look at the process of medication teaching before discharge. The results indicated that the teaching process was not standardized on the nursing units. As a result the information regarding medications on patient care referral forms for patients going to long-term care facilities or home health agencies was often inadequate. Continuity of care was not being provided. The issue was then referred to the patient education committee to standardize the process. It was decided that the function was the primary nurse's responsibility.

A reporting mechanism is essential for integrating into the overall hospital quality assurance program. Each institution will have its own structure. Continuing care and social work programs may be part of the clinical support quality assurance within the acute care setting. This structure facilitates reporting outcomes to the appropriate committees. In this way the results of quality assurance activities will be shared with others, and this will increase awareness of the discharge planning process.

RISK MANAGEMENT

"Risk management is a process whereby risk to the hospital and all who are associated with or served by it are evaluated and controlled in order to reduce or prevent future loss."[6] Malpractice or professional liability is often the focus of risk management.

The increased emphasis on discharge planning and its role under PPS increases the risk of liability. In addition, the kinds of care being delivered in settings outside the acute care hospital increase the responsibility for the discharge planner to adequately plan for these services. Patients being discharged with I.V. antibiotics, chemotherapy, total parenteral and enteral nutrition programs, and home ventilator care all require in-depth knowledgeable planning.

The risk for malpractice in discharge planning is apparent. The discharge planning manager must establish procedures for safe delivery of care and see that they are followed and carefully documented.

In instances when services are not available to meet needs, patients and families, as well as the physician, must be informed. The discharge planner must also explain and document what the services will and will not provide. The discharge planner must accurately represent the services expected.

Another area for risk to the institution is financial loss for the days that patients remain when they cannot be cared for elsewhere. The discharge planner must be totally aware of hospital policy, and document the problems in transfer as well as the decisions made by patient, family, and physician.

Risk management has taken on a new emphasis for the discharge planning manager. There are few precedents, and the events of the future will be the testing ground. Working closely with hospital legal counsel is a necessary strategy in program management.

CONCLUSION

Management of a discharge planning program has unique challenges. It requires coordination both within the institution and with agencies in the community. Objectives that coincide with the mission of the organization form the structure for the ongoing program. Policies and procedures must be developed that incorporate regulations and guidelines from accrediting and reimbursement sources. To monitor the quality of service provided, standards must be developed against which performance can be measured. Statistics are necessary to measure activities and project trends and to provide documentation for change. Computerization of discharge planning data is advantageous if the institution's data information system is able to support the discharge planning program needs.

Principles of management that emphasize communication will provide guidance to the discharge planning manager. The discharge planning manager should use the resources of peers through state and national continuity of care organizations for support. The task is to provide a flexible program that is responsive to the changing health care system. The rewards are a cost-effective program that provides quality continuity of care for patients and that is involved in changing the health care system.

NOTES

1. *Federal Register* 51, no. 116 (Tuesday, June 17, 1986): 22042–52.
2. Laura Mae Douglas and Em Olivia Bevis, *Nursing Management and Leadership in Action* (St. Louis: C.V. Mosby Co., 1983), p. 46.
3. Ronald G. Capelle, *Changing Human Systems* (Toronto: International Human Systems Institute, 1979), p. 135.
4. Massachusetts Chapter, National Association of Social Workers, Massachusetts Association of Hospital Social Work Directors, Boston Regional Continuing Care Nurses, and Massachusetts Continuing Care Association.
5. Bruce Pinchbeck, "Computers in Discharge Planning Management—The Basics" (tape) (San Antonio, Tex.: American Association for Continuity of Care, 1985).
6. Claire Gavin Meisenheimer, *Quality Assurance: A Complete Guide to Effective Programs* (Rockville, Md.: Aspen Publishers, 1985), p. 170.

REFERENCES

Capelle, Ronald G. *Changing Human Systems*. Toronto: International Human Systems Institute, 1979.
Craig, Sarah. "Hospital Administrators and Discharge Planners Discuss Discharge Planning to Home Care." *Baton* 2, no. 2 (Fall 1985), pp. 3–27.
Douglass, Laura Mae, and Bevis, Em Olivia. *Nursing Management and Leadership in Action*. 4th ed. St. Louis: C.V. Mosby Co., 1983.

Finkler, Steven A. *Budgeting Concepts for Nurse Managers*. Orlando, Fla.: Grune & Stratton, 1984.

Gillies, Du Ann. *Nursing Management: A Systems Approach*. Philadelphia: W.B. Saunders Co., 1982.

Hanson, Patricia C. *Management Systems for the Discharge Planning Professional*. Eagan, Minn.: Health Care Management Services, 1985.

Kennedy, Marily Moats. *Powerbase: How to Build It How to Keep It*. New York: Macmillan, 1984.

Liebler, Joan G., Levine, Ruth E., and Duvitz, Hyman L. *Management Principles for Health Professionals*. Rockville, Md.: Aspen Publishers, 1984.

McClelland, Eleanor; Kelly, Kathleen; and Buckwalter, Kathleen G. *Advancing the Concept of Discharge Planning*. Orlando, Fla.: Grune & Stratton, 1985.

McCoakey, Dale D. *How to Manage by Results*. 4th ed. New York: AMACOM Book Division, American Management Association, 1983.

McKeehan, Kathleen M. *Continuing Care: A Multidisciplinary Approach to Discharge Planning*. St. Louis: C.V. Mosby Co., 1981.

Marriner, Ann. *Guide to Nursing Management*. St. Louis: C.V. Mosby Co., 1984.

Meisenheimer, Claire Gavin. *Quality Assurance. A Complete Guide to Effective Programs*. Rockville, Md.: Aspen Publishers, 1985.

Peters, Thomas J., and Waterman, Robert H., Jr. *In Search of Excellence*. New York: Warner Books, 1982.

Stone, Sandra; Frisich, Shawn C.; Jordan, Shelby B; Berger, Marie S.; and Elhart, Dorothy. *Management for Nurses: A Multidisciplinary Approach*. St. Louis: C.V. Mosby Co., 1984.

Chapter 5

The Process of Discharge Planning

Sally Anne McCarthy

Chapter

The Process of Discharge Planning

5

Owing to more rigorous monitoring of health care by regulatory agencies and third party payers, there has been a tremendous increase in the attention given to discharge planning and continuity of care both in the literature and in various health care settings. Diagnosis-related group (DRG)-based reimbursement and demands for cost containment in the health care field have placed tremendous stress on patients, families, health professionals, and community resources. Procedures once carried out in the hospital setting are now being done only in an ambulatory setting in order for the patient to receive reimbursement. Hospital stays are shorter, patients have less recuperative time in the hospital, and thus greater demands are placed on patients, families, hospital staff, and community resources. Quality assurance standards require hospitals to provide ongoing monitoring and evaluation of the quality and appropriateness of patient care.[1]

TERMINOLOGY

The terms discharge planning, continuing care, and continuity of care, although frequently used interchangeably, are defined somewhat differently by various authors and indeed should be clearly delineated.

Continuing care has been defined by LaMontagne and McKeehan[2] as "a hospital based program which coordinates assessment, planning and follow-up procedures by providing a multidisciplinary team approach to patients with posthospital needs." Discharge planning is frequently used synonymously with the above definition and has been defined as a "centralized, coordinated program developed by a hospital to ensure that each patient has a planned program for needed continuing or follow up care."[3]

The American Nurses' Association, however, has provided a broader definition, defining discharge planning as "that part of the continuity of care process which is designed to prepare the patient or client for the next phase of care and to assist in making any necessary arrangements for that phase of care, whether it be self care, care by family members or care by an organized health care provider."[4] Thus discharge planning should occur in any health care setting where patients and families require preparation for receiving health care at the next level of care. Buckwalter[5] defines discharge planning as "the process by which the goal of continuity of care is attained." Continuity of care, as defined by McKeehan,[6] is "the term applied to the coordinated delivery of health services on a continuum." The continuum includes the delivery of health care services in the home through self-care, or with the assistance of families or home health agencies. It includes ambulatory settings, such as neighborhood clinics, private practices, and emergency departments, and extends to inpatient hospital care, rehabilitation, or chronic care facilities as well as hospices. The patients' needs and desires for health services will vary considerably, depending on where they are on the continuum at any given time.

PHILOSOPHY

In order to achieve the goal of continuity of care, the patient and health care professionals from various disciplines and health care settings must work together in a coordinated effort to achieve mutually agreed upon goals. This involves a multidisciplinary approach to individualized assessment of the patient's health care needs as well as patient involvement in the decision-making process. It is the responsibility of each health care professional involved in the provision of the patient's care to participate in the discharge planning process. Communication, collaboration, coordination, and documentation are all essential components of this participation.

All patients have a right to discharge planning that will prepare them to receive the health care services they need at the appropriate level of care. For some it may be written instructions for the medication regimen and follow-up medical appointments. Others will require the services of a community health nurse to monitor the medication regimen and assess pulmonary and nutritional status. Still others will require intricate planning with a multidisciplinary approach in order to meet their needs for continuity of care.

By involving the patient and family in the decision-making process, goals are mutually established and will be more realistic, and thus more readily attainable.[7] In contrast, patients who have no involvement in the decision making may feel powerless and manipulated.[8] Such feelings create anger and noncompliance, which is counterproductive in assisting patients to maintain or regain optimum health. The following case study will illustrate this issue.

Case Study

T. J., an 11-month-old male, was hospitalized since birth in a community hospital and transferred to a tertiary care hospital at 5 months of age for further studies because of severe chronic lung disease and failure to thrive. Both parents worked full time. There was a 2½-year-old male sibling in the home and the family lived approximately 90 miles from the hospital. Referral to social work was rejected by the parents, in that they repeatedly broke appointments with the worker and failed to follow through on suggestions such as applying for Supplemental Security Income (SSI) or Medicaid.

Visiting was infrequent, and hospital staff assessed minimal nurturing and interest in caregiving on the part of both parents. In view of this and because the insurance did not provide adequate home care services for a ventilator-dependent child, the health care professionals involved in T. J.'s care "decided" that continued acute hospital care was the only option until he could be weaned from both ventilator and oxygen. When the parents were informed of this plan they offered no resistance.

During the next 3 months the parents' visits became more infrequent, were always unannounced, and often included angry outbursts, particularly by the mother. In addition, T. J.'s developmental delay became increasingly evident and he began ruminating.

Several multidisciplinary meetings were held, and the parents were belatedly included as part of the team and encouraged to become actively involved in T. J.'s plan of care. A new social worker was assigned to work with the parents, and gradually the parents were able to assume their role in his feeding protocol. Alternative plans were discussed with the family with differing potential discharge dates. Mrs. J. subsequently made plans to stop working outside of the home in order to bring T. J. home with oxygen at an earlier date than originally planned. Both parents expressed realistic concerns, but with the supportive services available in the hospital and community, they were eager to assume their roles as parents.

In this case study T. J.'s parents were initially denied their right to be actively involved in discharge planning. The mother had been heard to angrily state that she had no control over her life. However, once the parents became actively involved and received adequate support, T. J.'s discharge plan met his health care needs both in respect to quality and cost-effectiveness.

Coulton et al.[9] found, in their study of patient involvement in decision making, that the degree of satisfaction with a discharge plan was directly related to the level of involvement of the patient.

DISCHARGE PLANNING PROCESS

As with the nursing process, discharge planning involves assessing, planning, implementing, and evaluating.[10] See Figure 5-1. Although the four components follow a logical progression, there will often be two or more components in operation at any given time. The process is cyclic, and between and among the components there is constant movement.[11]

Assessment

Steffl and Eide[12] have identified assessment as the most determining factor in discharge planning. Assessing and identifying a patient's current and anticipated physical and psychosocial needs, his or her support net-

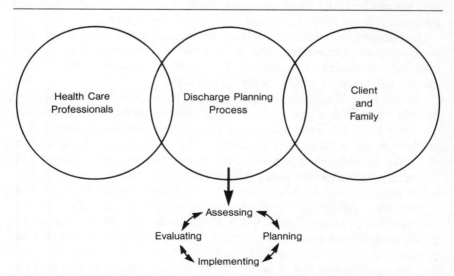

Figure 5-1 The Discharge Planning Process. *Source:* Adapted courtesy of Teresa Ahmann.

works, and his or her home environment will provide essential data for determining on which level of the continuum the patient will receive health care services. It will often indicate the need for a transition to another provider of health care, whether this is in the direction of self-care or of more intense services. Regardless of the direction taken on the continuum, the patient will undoubtedly experience some degree of stress as the provider of health care services is altered.

Comprehensive assessment is obtained by the communication and collaboration of the various health care professionals involved in the patient's care. Although any number of disciplines may be involved, the physician, nurse, social worker, and patient are the most frequently involved. It is an ongoing, dynamic process that involves the skills derived from the special body of knowledge of each discipline involved.

It is the physician who must admit and discharge patients and take the initial responsibility for a discharge plan. Before or at the time of hospital admission the physician is expected to determine an anticipated length of stay and to identify problems that will hinder a timely discharge. The physician knows the primary and any associated diagnoses that affect the patient's health, prognosis, and functional limitations. As soon as potential problems are identified, other health care professionals need to be consulted to provide needed services. The discharge plan, although implemented by other professionals, is signed by the physician for both legal and reimbursement purposes. Whether physicians actively assume their role for initiating discharge plans or not, they play an integral role in the process.

As discussed in Chapter 1, nursing's role in assessing for planning for continuity of care was recognized in 1966, in the National League for Nursing's published Statement of Continuity of Nursing Care.[13]

> Planning for continuing nursing care is initiated when the patient is first seen by a nurse, wherever the nurse is practicing. It begins with an assessment of present nursing needs and the development of a nursing care plan to meet present needs. It includes anticipatory evaluation of future needs, and progresses to a referral to the appropriate agency or institution which can meet those needs.

The nurse's body of knowledge provides specific skills in assessing physical status, levels of care, self-care needs, home environment, and patient or family health education needs.[14] Their 24-hour availability places nurses in a unique position within the hospital setting to assess needs of patient and family that might not be evident during the 8 A.M. to 5 P.M.

Monday-through-Friday workday. For example, family members may visit only on the evening shift, and pertinent assessments might significantly alter the discharge plan.

Social workers' unique body of knowledge lies in their expertise in interviewing, assessing needs and resources, counseling the patient and family as they make decisions, and linking them with appropriate community support services.[15] Social workers have expertise in making psychosocial assessments of the patient's situation, which is essential to any discharge plan. Their discipline is also oriented to working with families and systems.

The importance of the patient's role in the decision-making process has been discussed within the philosophy of this chapter. Coulton[16] has described the ideal in discharge planning as a decision-making process. She defines four conditions that create a climate conducive to exploring alternatives and a healthy decision-making process. These include adequate time, hope, social support, and freedom of choice.

Neither the patient's condition nor the hospital environment may allow for full implementation of such an ideal. However, both professionals and hospitals must strive to help patients and families explore possible alternatives and participate in the decision making within whatever limitations exist.

Although expertise and roles overlap—particularly between social work and nursing—there are distinct advantages in this. As health professionals they must perceive their roles as complementary, and they must collaborate as colleagues in providing effective discharge planning. Each discipline has information that is invaluable to the other, and neither can be the sole determinant of the patient's discharge plan.[17] Their common goal is a comprehensive assessment that will facilitate a timely and appropriate discharge plan. Inaccurate or incomplete assessments will lead to partial or unsatisfactory recommendations that in turn result in poor decisions. In contrast, comprehensive, multidisciplinary assessments that include patient involvement have the potential for the best possible decisions.[18]

Recent changes in the health care delivery system have placed greater emphasis on hospital preadmission screening.[19] Those hospitals determined to streamline the process and improve the likelihood of third party reimbursement have revised forms and developed policies in order to expedite a timely discharge and identify factors that affect the patient's discharge. Physicians who plan elective admissions need to provide both primary and secondary diagnoses, an anticipated length of stay, previous hospital admissions, expected disposition of patient after discharge, reimbursement information, and identification of various resources needed during the hospitalization. Thorough assessment and documentation on admission avoids duplication of efforts on the part of social work, business office, utilization review, and discharge planning. Duplication is costly to the hospital and irritating to the patient, who is repeatedly asked the same questions.

Cunningham,[20] Rasmussen,[21] McCarthy,[22] Kitto and Dale,[23] and others have developed screening criteria to identify patients who will require special attention in discharge planning. Such assessment criteria serve as an excellent discharge management tool to assess potential problems and identify the need for referrals in a timelier manner. Screening tools should be used on admission and updated throughout the hospitalization as new data become available through the collaboration of various disciplines. It is advisable to develop tools that will screen problems that are pertinent to a specific patient population. For example, screening criteria in an adult acute medical unit will differ from criteria used on a rehabilitation unit or a pediatric unit. This enables the screen to be more compact and easier to use. Unit-based screening tools might be developed from an overall discharge management screening tool that identifies the risks of the entire hospital population and the screening policy of the discharge planning program or department.

Planning

Planning begins with the formulation of the medical plan of care and the nursing care plan. The more comprehensive the assessment, the more likely appropriate referrals will be made in a timely manner. For example, the admission of a woman with carcinoma of the colon, who will probably have a colostomy after surgery, would alert the staff to the need for a referral to social work as well as to the clinical nursing specialist. Patient teaching and the provision of psychosocial support will begin preoperatively and thus, it is hoped, expedite discharge.

Planning will require identification of all necessary inhospital and community referrals. It will identify plans that need to be carried out by patient, family, and all involved health care providers. It is important that as patient needs are identified, the appropriate person (health care professional, patient, or family) who will be accountable for meeting these needs be identified. Establishing and documenting accountability will enhance implementation of the plan.

In the hospital setting daily physician and nursing rounds provide the means for at least briefly addressing discharge plans. Multidisciplinary rounds should be held at least weekly in order to reassess patient needs and patient readiness for discharge. The plan is altered whenever indicated, as continued assessments provide new data and identify the need for a change in the original plan. For example, if the original plan is for home care and continued assessments raise doubts as to the feasibility of home care, an alternate plan should be made. Possibly the family is having difficulty learning the care and an alternate plan should be initiated.

In addition to the weekly multidisciplinary rounds, in which all or most patients are discussed, one or more individual predischarge conferences may be needed for the patient with complex needs. All health care professionals involved in the patient's care should be involved in such a conference. An initial meeting of health professionals without patient and family might be advisable in order to explore strengths, deficits, and the feasibility of specific plans. An example of this would be a meeting in which professionals could discuss the feasibility of home ventilator care for a patient. Before involving the family in such a plan, the medical stability and financial support for home care should be established. However, all subsequent meetings must include patient and family.

Hollingsworth and Sokol[24] describe the purpose of such a conference as being to discuss posthospital care, finalize plans for discharge, evaluate patient understanding of care needs, and assess the emotional effect of the illness on the patient and family. Their cardiology patients had evidenced increased anxiety or depression before discharge and had difficulty recalling the medical information provided them during hospitalization. By having a conference two or three days before discharge, such anxieties could be decreased.

In planning home care for a patient with complex needs (for example, a ventilator-dependent patient) such conferences are invaluable. I have found that they:

- involve patient and family in decision making and thus assure more commitment to the plan;
- enable patient and staff to review the status of the plan;
- provide a forum for patient and staff to discuss concerns they have regarding discharge;
- develop patient confidence, for example, in reviewing how much they have learned or accomplished in past weeks;
- enable community resource people, such as from a home health agency, to attend and become active participants in the discharge plan; and
- develop confidence of the health care professionals in the likelihood of the discharge plan's success.

Implementation

Implementation is the phase wherein the individualized discharge plan, mutually chosen by patient, family, and health care providers, is activated and carried out. It involves mobilization of appropriate and available resources that will help the patient obtain needed health care services at the next level of care. It includes counseling, discharge teaching, ordering needed equipment, and making appropriate follow-up appointments and community referrals.

As the plan is implemented, it must always be reassessed and evaluated, for it is only by reassessing and evaluating the process as it evolves that one can test the original plan and make necessary alterations before discharge. This will be illustrated by the following case study.

Case Study

Mrs. J. was a 79-year-old widow with a partial left hemiparesis and chronic lung disease. She had been living alone for four years since her husband died and had remained self-sufficient until this recent hospitalization for a stroke that resulted in the hemiparesis.

Her only child was a son who lived several states away. Both son and daughter-in-law were professionals who worked full-time. Mrs. J.'s relationship with her son had been close but manipulative over the years. She and her daughter-in-law had maintained a cordial but somewhat distant relationship.

The discharge plan established was to move Mrs. J. to her son's home, which all three persons professed as their preference. Supportive services, such as nursing and physical therapy, would be available from the local home health agency. A homemaker would be used part-time while the son and daughter-in-law worked.

Mrs. J.'s son and daughter-in-law were spending the three weeks before discharge learning about her care and preparing for the move. Mr. J. developed a recurrent ulcer that required medical care. His wife manifested little interest or commitment to learning how to care for her mother-in-law.

Considerable counseling of all three persons, as well as reassessment and evaluation of the discharge plan, indicated a need for an alternative plan. Mr. J. realized that although he loved and wanted desperately to care for his mother, bringing her into his home would seriously jeopardize his marriage and health because of the stresses involved.

Further counseling with Mrs. J. enabled her to accept that although she wanted to be with her son, she also wanted to avoid being a burden and an "unwanted guest" during her last years of life. A nursing home was located near the son's home, and the discharge plan was altered before discharge. Mrs. J. left the hospital somewhat apprehensive about her new environment but was reassured that her son and daughter-in-law would be close enough for frequent visits and that occasional passes to their home would be possible.

Patient Teaching

Patient teaching is a major consideration in any health care setting and an essential component of the discharge planning process. Depending on the setting, the needs of the patient, and the resources available, it will be done by staff nurse, primary nurse, clinical specialist, patient educator, dietitian, or rehabilitation therapist.

The initial steps in patient teaching are to assess the patient's readiness for learning and the patient's learning needs. This is a complex task, in that cues regarding patient readiness are often difficult to accurately interpret.

Patients in any health care setting present with diverse levels of knowledge and skills.[25] Those with a new illness may have little or erroneous information about their condition. Those who have lived with a chronic illness for a number of years may be knowledgeable about their condition or may have erroneous information as well as a long history of noncompliance.

A patient's readiness to learn is significantly modified by his or her emotions, and the impact of an illness crisis will cause some degree of both emotional and cognitive regression.[26] The degree of emotional response to any illness varies. Considerable time and effort are wasted if education is thrust on clients when they are emotionally unable to assimilate it or are not in need of that particular aspect of teaching. In this time of shortened hospital stays, health professionals must be prepared to teach acutely ill patients highly technical information in less time than ever before. Yet learning will be determined by their state of readiness as well as their predisposition toward learning.[27]

Careful assessment of the patient's ability to read and comprehend is essential before determining the teaching method or content. Literacy cannot be assumed, nor is grade level attainment an accurate gauge of reading ability. Patients often devise clever ways to conceal their lack of reading ability.

Doak et al. estimate that 23 million American adults may not be able to comprehend what health professionals are talking about.[28] They are labeled functionally illiterate and may not be able to comprehend either written instructions or audiovisual aids. Van Hoozer et al. state that at least another 40 million adults function at or below the level of marginal literacy.[29]

Formulas such as the Cloze method are helpful in assessing reading comprehension. In this method every fifth word is deleted from a passage and the reader is given the task of filling in the blanks. Reading comprehension can also be assessed by having the patient read the material aloud and then provide his or her interpretation and understanding. The use of open-ended questions is helpful in determining comprehension.

In planning a teaching strategy one should consider the following steps:

• Teach the smallest amount possible to accomplish the goal.
• Make your point as vividly as possible.
• Have the client restate or demonstrate the information.
• Review repeatedly.[30]

An organized teaching plan or checklist should be developed for specific conditions. Any teaching plan or checklist must also identify the appropriate teaching methods to be used, for example, discussion, instructional materials, demonstrations, and return demonstrations. This will provide standardization of patient teaching and will communicate what nurses need to teach and what the patient has learned. Giving patients a copy of the teaching plan to take home for later reference will help to reduce their anxiety and possibly lessen the chance that they will have to be readmitted. A copy should be maintained for the medical record and another copy should be sent to the clinic or home health agency that will follow the patient. In today's climate, documentation of patient teaching is essential from an institutional liability perspective.

Discharge is a time of stress and patients often have their minds on other concerns, which makes verbal instructions inadequate. Discharge dates are frequently changed or not communicated by the physician. Consequently patient teachers find themselves teaching someone who is making plans for going home rather than concentrating on learning.

In developing written instructions it is essential to consider the visual impairments that many elderly patients have as well as the fact that many patients will be either functional or marginal illiterates. Thus teaching tools and home care instructions should be directed at or below the eighth grade reading level.[31] The use of pictures, diagrams, and audiovisuals will be helpful.

Readability formulas should also be considered when developing or purchasing written materials. The Minnesota Educational Computing

Consortium (MECC) has developed a program for the Apple computer called "MECC School Utilities, Volume 2," which enables one to enter any text and calculate the readability level within seconds.[32]

All teaching materials should be carefully previewed and evaluated before being used. Frequently this is done by colleagues and followed by a trial use by a select group of patients. Such evaluation is helpful in determining suitability for the intended use, in that the materials can be revised before being used extensively. Reviews of print and nonprint materials can be obtained through AVLINE, a computer-based listing and description of available audiovisual materials that is supported by the National Library of Medicine,[33] as well as in many professional journals.

Patient education must address knowledge of the disease process, medications, diet, and activity. It is important to stress *why* medications, diet, and restrictions in activities are important and the risk and possible complications that may result if instructions are not followed. Patients may need to develop manual skills, such as self-injection, self-catheterization, or changing a colostomy pouch. For some it will be essential to practice problem-solving or coping skills—for example, "What will you do if your tracheostomy plugs and you're riding in the car?" "What will you do if you forget to take your blood pressure medication for two or three days?"

The use of checklists, teaching plans, and written home care instructions will facilitate documentation of the teaching that occurred and what knowledge the patient verbalized or demonstrated before discharge.

When patient education will require several teaching sessions, it is helpful to contract with the patient or family members who must learn the care. This helps to clarify expectations and actively involves the patient or family in making a commitment to learn the necessary care. Having helped to select the times for teaching sessions, they should be held accountable for fulfilling the agreement. If the teaching does not progress as planned, the discharge plan should be reassessed. Some families are overwhelmed, and although they may sincerely want the patient home, an alternative plan, such as nursing home placement, will be needed, at least temporarily. In some instances the teaching could be completed and reinforced by a visiting nurse. In the latter case it will be important to make the referral early in order to provide follow-up immediately after discharge. Continuity of teaching will be provided if the visiting nurse has a copy of the checklist or teaching plan that clearly communicates what the patient has been taught and what teaching remains to be done. It is suggested that the reader refer to specific readings on teaching and learning.

Equipment

Nurses, as well as physicians, physical therapists, and occupational therapists, are the professionals most likely to identify the need for equipment that will make the patient more comfortable or functional or that will facilitate home care. Hospital beds, wheelchairs, bedside commodes, overhead trapezes, assistive devices, suction machines, oxygen, and nebulizers have been used in the home for some time. With today's high-technology home care, increasingly complex equipment is being used in the home to provide ventilatory support, dialysis, intravenous therapy, and parenteral nutrition. Early identification of equipment needs is essential to avoid delays in discharge.

Before preparing any patient for home care, one must determine what options are available financially. State Medicaid programs, HMOs, and even private insurance policies vary considerably in their limitations. Some policies will not provide any reimbursement for equipment or oxygen, whereas others will pay as much as 80 percent. When patients will be responsible for any portion of equipment costs, they must be made aware of this well before discharge. If assessed early, the discharge planner will have time to search for foundations or associations that might provide assistance. The selection of vendors may be affected in that some are higher priced than others, and some are more likely to accept patients who are unable to pay for the equipment.

Many HMOs and third party payers have contracts with specific vendors who will offer them discounts. The discharge planner must be knowledgeable regarding such restrictions, since the patient may be held responsible for the bill if the equipment is ordered from a different company. However, if the discharge planner has valid concerns about any company known to provide unsafe or inadequate services, these concerns should be made known and perhaps another company could be selected.

Third party payers are becoming increasingly open to negotiations regarding coverage for equipment and other home care services. If one can document that the equipment is needed and that home care is less costly, exceptions are often made. It is, of course, easier to negotiate if the prognosis is favorable and the need for the equipment is not for long-term, chronic, maintenance care. Although time-consuming, negotiating such exceptions can be most rewarding to both the patient and the discharge planner.

Hartsell and Ward[34] have devised a checklist for selecting and evaluating home care equipment vendors for pediatric patients. They identify a number of criteria, such as 24-hour availability and the servicing or replacement of equipment in emergencies. It is equally important that vendors provide feedback to the discharge planner regarding problems they encounter in the home.

A home evaluation, before discharge, may be indicated to assess the general layout of the home and its ability to accommodate special equipment. The evaluation might also include an assessment of available electrical outlets, a telephone for emergency use in or near the patient's room, adequate screening or insulation, the presence of pets that would be hazardous to a patient with respiratory disease, and the presence of heavy smokers in the home who would jeopardize the patient's health and safety.

Patients and families must be instructed on the use and maintenance of equipment as well as in how to perform appropriate emergency interventions. Vendors should provide instruction on delivery or at least before discharge. Equipment often varies from that used in the hospital, and regardless of how well the hospital nurses have instructed the patient or family, the home setting is entirely different and therefore anxiety-producing. Sharing the hospital's teaching checklists will enhance continuity in the patient's education.

Referrals

Shorter lengths of stay place stress on patients and health care professionals, making follow-up a more crucial step in the discharge planning process. If patients are being discharged earlier, it is essential to prevent their being discharged ill-prepared and prematurely. As patients go home earlier from hospitals their care plans will be more complex, necessitating careful medical follow-up. Thus patients should be given specific appointments with dates and times rather than the vague instruction "Call Dr. Jones's office for an appointment in two weeks."

Referrals to community agencies, such as home health agencies, become equally crucial in that nurses can make home visits to complete patient education or confirm that the hospital teaching has been effective and that the discharge plan is being implemented. If problems are identified, it is hoped that they can be resolved and that readmission can be averted.

To expedite discharge planning and encourage nurses to make community health referrals, it is important to establish criteria for identifying patients who need referrals. Forms should be developed that will improve efficiency and assist nurses in completing an objective patient assessment, followed by a care plan designed to meet the needs identified. The goal should be a clear, succinct referral that is multidimensional and relevant. To provide services more promptly, and thus enhance continuity of care, the referral should be initiated by telephone and then followed up in writing.

Developing a discharge planning manual for each patient unit will also streamline the process. Such a manual might include hospital policies and procedures related to discharge as well as samples of tools, for example, screening criteria, checklists, and standardized home care instructions. Equally important would be a list of available community resources and a sample of a well-written home health agency referral.

Evaluation

The final step in the process is evaluation. Muenchow and Carlson[35] describe outcome criteria as the most effective method for evaluating discharge planning models. Individual discharge plans and the overall discharge planning program must be evaluated in order to ensure that high-quality continuity of care is provided for patients.

In evaluating individual discharge plans, objective criteria need to be developed in order to measure the plan's success in meeting specific patient needs. This can be accomplished by follow-up of all patients or a predetermined percentage of patients. Including a follow-up form (feedback sheet) with each referral to a home health agency, with a length of time specified for its completion and return, is one method. A copy of the feedback sheet should be shared with the physician who is following the patient. Sharing another copy with the staff who originated the referral allows them to evaluate their discharge plan. It also provides considerable personal satisfaction in that it enables them to see the patient's progress.

Telephone follow-up of patients and families and of home health agencies is another means of evaluating individual discharge plans. Were patients adequately instructed? Were patient needs appropriately identified in the hospital setting? Was the input of all members of the health care team adequate? Were other problems identified by the patient or home health agency that were not assessed in the hospital? Was the discharge plan implemented? Was the home health agency able to provide the services requested or promised? Is the patient functioning at the most independent level possible? By providing evaluations of individual discharge plans one can ensure the safety of patients and revise plans in order to improve the ability to meet future patient needs.

Periodic program evaluation will help to modify institutional planning, such as the patient education program or the development of hospital resources, to meet patient needs. Rossen[36] cites the need for regular evaluation of referral sources to ensure timeliness, appropriateness, and quality. By identifying gaps in community services, hospitals are developing new programs, for example, their own equipment companies, home health agencies, or day-care centers.

By ongoing evaluation of both individual discharge plans and the program itself, health professionals can help to ensure high-quality continuity of care.

KNOWLEDGE NEEDED BY THE DISCHARGE PLANNER

Legislation and Regulations

Discharge planning nurses and social workers have a responsibility to be knowledgeable about regulations that affect discharge planning. Keeping up to date on current or proposed legislation and regulations requires consistent reading of appropriate journals and publications. Membership in their respective local and national professional organizations will perhaps provide them with an even greater opportunity to remain knowledgeable. As advocates for the patient within the health care system and for the institution or agency employing them, they must be highly skilled in helping patients gain access to care that is both appropriate and cost-effective.

In many metropolitan areas local groups of professionals involved in providing continuity of care meet regularly for the purpose of networking and attending educational programs that keep members up to date on resources and legislative issues that affect continuity of care. Whether formal or informal, such meetings provide an excellent opportunity for problem solving and sharing. Members often represent hospital discharge planners, professionals from home health agencies, and third party payers.

The American Association for Continuity of Care (AACC) is a national multidisciplinary organization that provides members with current information regarding legislative and regulatory activity that affects continuity of care. Members are encouraged to keep the Washington office informed of concerns on continuity of care issues. Qualified speakers with expertise have testified at congressional hearings, and AACC has joined coalitions of various professional organizations in order to effect changes in the health care system.

All too often professionals grumble among themselves regarding the constraints imposed on them by regulations. They underestimate how valuable their input could be for those who are writing the legislation. As individuals and as members of a professional organization, they have a responsibility to provide input into the development and evaluation of various regulations that affect their patients. By making their views known to local and national associations, discharge planners are able to influence legislation that affects health care.

Legislators are required to make decisions on a wide variety of issues and cannot possibly be experts on each issue. Consequently they need the experts to identify issues and provide the data that support the need for legislation and regulations. Once legislation has been passed, the legislator then needs objective feedback from those who are implementing the legislation and those who are affected by it.[37]

Government Insurance Programs

Medicare is a health insurance program for people 65 years of age or older, for certain disabled people, and for those who have end-stage renal disease. It is a federal program administered by the Health Care Financing Administration and is thus national in scope and uniform in eligibility requirements and benefits. It has two parts, commonly referred to as Part A and Part B.

Medicare Part A is hospital insurance that provides payment for medically necessary hospital care and, after a hospitalization, for limited inpatient care in a skilled nursing facility. It also pays for skilled home care services provided by a certified home health agency.

Medicare Part B is supplementary medical insurance that can help pay for necessary physician services, outpatient hospital services and therapies, drugs administered by a physician, supplies, and skilled home health services. A monthly premium must be paid for coverage under Part B. Since the 1972 amendments to the Social Security Act,[38] enrollment in Part B is automatic, with provisions being made for those who want to decline it.

Medicaid is a federally aided, state-administered program that assists some people who cannot pay for health care. There are no age restrictions. Although subject to federal guidelines, each state determines its eligibility requirements as well as the scope of benefits provided. Consequently there is a wide variation from state to state regarding services provided. Generally the patient's income is below a state-designated poverty level or medical expenses are high enough in relation to family income to make the patient eligible.

Medicare does not pay the full cost of some services provided. If the patient's income is low enough to enable him or her to qualify for Medicaid, the Medicaid program in some states may pay the amount Medicare does not cover, and it may pay for some health care expenses not covered by Medicare.

Hospital discharge planners must be knowledgeable regarding Medicare and Medicaid coverage in order to assist patients and families. Understanding restrictions such as the deductible, the copayment restriction, and the upper limit allowed under Medicare will enable them to make informed decisions. Relying on Medicare provisions alone can leave families with extensive hospital bills. At the same time it can seriously limit their alternatives in discharge planning.

Before the passage of Medicare and Medicaid as amendments to the Social Security Act in 1965, most home care services provided to the elderly were for subacute nursing care for patients with chronic conditions. Voluntary visiting nurse agencies or public health agencies provided most home care. Payment was provided by welfare agencies or privately on a sliding scale, with fees subsidized by charitable organizations.[39] Because Medicare was based on a medical model for acute care, eligibility for home care also became based on a medical model, rather than on that of providing supportive or custodial services. Although no previous hospital stay is required to receive a home health care benefit, the following conditions must be met:

- Care must be ordered by a physician.
- The patient must be homebound.
- The need for care must be intermittent.
- The care needed must be "skilled" care.

For a patient to qualify for skilled care in the home under Medicare's definition, the services must be rendered by a registered nurse, physical therapist, or speech pathologist. Other insurers' criteria for home care eligibility vary. For Blue Cross and Blue Shield, if home care is "in lieu of hospitalization," then the patient qualifies for reimbursement. Medicare, Medicaid, "the Blues," and commercial insurers are currently changing their coverage criteria for reimbursable home health services. Some insurers are increasing the kinds and types of services covered, whereas others are becoming more restrictive.

For Medicare to pay for care in a skilled nursing facility, "skilled care" must also be required. This skilled care requires the services of a registered nurse, physicians, and possibly therapists for rehabilitation. The patient requires continuous observation and supervision of treatment goals. This skilled care must never be confused with long-term custodial or maintenance care.

There are four recognized levels of care, progressing from most to least complicated medical needs. They are as follows:

1. *Acute.* The patient is in the most serious or critical stage of illness and requires hospitalization for diagnostic workup and implementation of a treatment plan.
2. *Skilled.* The patient's treatment plan requires ongoing care carried out by a physician, a nurse, or registered therapists. The patient needs rehabilitation therapy and must show potential for improvement or have a deteriorating condition that requires skilled nursing care.
3. *Intermediate.* The patient is almost self-sufficient, needs some support and assistance, but is expected to make progress and possibly go home. Rehabilitation by skilled therapists is complete, but nursing supervision is needed for some activities.
4. *Custodial.* The patient needs assistance with the activities of daily living, but no improvement is expected and therapists have apparently accomplished all they can.

Both Medicare and Medicaid fund acute and skilled levels, within specific limitations, whereas only Medicaid would fund intermediate or custodial levels of care.[40]

The Supplemental Security Income (SSI) program is a federal income maintenance program for the aged, blind, and disabled. Patients who meet eligibility criteria receive monthly SSI payments based on family income. Discharge planners should be aware of this program in order to refer patients to the hospital social worker for assistance. Application may be made at any Social Security office.

Private Insurance

Discharge planners must be aware of their patients' insurance coverage. They must maintain a dialogue with reviewers within the insurance plan. Private insurance varies from policy to policy regarding coverage for hospital and skilled nursing facility care. When patients and families can be relieved of the worry about medical costs, their sense of well-being can be affected in a positive way.

Although no health professional wants to be forced to select follow-up care according to what is covered by health insurance, the reality is that insurance coverage does indeed have a tremendous influence on the alternatives available for continuity of care. Discharge planners must be aware of benefits and limitations before they make recommendations to any patient or family. It is unconscionable for any health professional to add to the patient's or family's grief and guilt by offering a discharge plan that will be financially unattainable.

Thus the discharge planner must have a close working relationship with personnel in the business office as well as contacts in individual insurance companies. Business or credit office personnel are primarily concerned with payment of the hospital bill and are usually not well versed in home care or long-term care issues. Although they can provide the discharge planner with some information and with the name and phone number of a contact person within the insurance company, the pertinent questions that need to be asked require a degree of clinical judgment.

An encouraging note has been the increasing number of insurance companies who are now employing registered nurses to manage individual cases. This enables the hospital discharge planner and the case manager to make clinical judgments while negotiating in the interest of more humane health care for the patient and cost containment for the insurance company. Although not always successful, the competent discharge planner will develop skills in appealing and negotiating, thus obtaining coverage for services not routinely covered. An increasing number of insurance companies have agreed to provide private duty nursing in the home when it has been proven to be less expensive than acute care hospitalization. The effective discharge planner will soon develop a reputation for being an advocate for quality cost-effective patient care that is in the best interest of the patient and the third party payer.

Barriers remain, however, in meeting the continuing care needs of patients of all ages. Insurance coverage is frequently limited to services that are restorative—those that will alleviate or cure an illness versus those that are custodial. The purpose is to avoid routine maintenance care, which is precisely what is so often needed to maintain the patient's health and independence.

Another barrier is that many policies include a maximum annual or lifetime benefit. With today's high technology a patient can easily approach this maximum limit before he or she is ready to use the home care benefit. A referral to social work would be indicated in order to assist the patient or family in applying for benefits, for example, Medicaid or SSI.

Providing holistic care means meeting patients' needs in all areas of their mental and physical well-being. Certainly in these times this means that one must also consider their financial health. Thus the discharge planner must be well versed in eligibility for such programs as SSI, Medicare, Medicaid, and Workmen's Compensation. Counseling clients about the importance of keeping all receipts of payments for medications, medical supplies, or tests may also prove invaluable to their financial, physical, and mental health.

Discharge planners must, of course, be knowledgeable regarding available services and resources that can benefit their patients and families. It is no small feat to remain up to date regarding federal, state, and local resources as well as religious, private, and other community resources. The availability and quality of resources will vary from one community to another, depending on economic factors, societal attitudes, and politics.[41] However, in order to refer patients to resources that are appropriate to their needs, the prudent discharge planner will devise a system whereby a resource list is readily available. It is essential to consider the characteristics of the patients and families, the hospital, and the community being served when developing a resource file or list.

With prospective payment and earlier discharge from hospitals, more patients may be referred to long-term facilities than in the past. The discharge planner must be certain that the skilled nursing facility can provide adequate care. An updated list of facilities that provide skilled, intermediate, or custodial care and whether or not they accept Medicare or Medicaid will save considerable time. Patient and family must be informed of any expenses for which they will be responsible.

Information about referral agencies that should always be considered include cost of services, payment sources accepted, special populations considered, specialties of the agency, expertise of their staff, specific limitations, and the usual length of time required to process an application.

Evaluation of the discharge plan has been discussed earlier in this chapter, including the use of a follow-up form with each referral to a home health agency. Families should also be encouraged to provide both positive and negative feedback to the discharge planner. Helping families work out problems for themselves, whenever possible, makes discharge planning more effective. Agencies may need to be made aware of problems, and those who developed the discharge plan need to be aware of any problems that could have been alleviated from their perspective. Good communication between the patient and family, the discharge planner, and the referral agency is needed to assure an easy transition from one level of care to another.

Networking within local, state, or national organizations will help to identify needs and gaps in services. Individual agencies and organizations will often attempt to meet existing needs that are identified for them by professionals and families.

Skills needed by the discharge planner are many and some have been alluded to previously in this chapter. Certainly the role requires the skills of an educator. Today more than ever patients and families need to be educated to maximize self-care. They need to understand what Medicare does and does not provide and what their supplemental policies may offer. The prospective reimbursement system makes it critical for them to know what alternative delivery methods are available.

Educating the entire hospital staff as well as the public regarding DRGs and the use of appropriate resources is an important role for all health professionals. Certainly the discharge planner has a vested interest in helping patients, families, hospital staff, and the general public understand that the thrust is to provide more efficient care, not just to rush them through a hasty discharge.

Communication skills are a vital component of any discharge planner's repertoire. Verbal and written communication is constantly required in order to collaborate with other health care professionals, patients, families, third party payers, and community agencies. Demands for productivity will be increased. Good documentation and devising appropriate tools and forms will all enhance effective discharge planning and productivity. Effective communication between the discharge planner and other members of the health care team within the hospital and community is essential to the success of discharge planning. All members of the team rely on collaboration to achieve the common goal of continuity of care. Discharge planners influence the behavior of all members of the health care team. By positively influencing their behavior, the discharge plan is coordinated as all members of the team carry out their roles.

Flexibility is always needed, since the discharge plan is continually being reassessed to meet newly identified needs. Sensitivity and intuitiveness regarding the stresses that patients, families, and colleagues are experiencing are essential in order to provide the support needed.

Because the role is that of educator, change agent, facilitator, consultant, and coordinator, certainly a degree of assertiveness is also required. The crux of success lies in the delicate balance of all of these qualities in order to maintain an alliance approach to attaining the goal of continuity of care.

Although the prevailing philosophy over the past few decades has been that everyone has the right to the best health care available, regardless of economic status, prospective reimbursement is challenging this philosophy.[42] Indeed many predict that there will be a two-tiered system of health care in the near future.

The prospective payment system supports a trend toward shorter hospitalizations and more reliance on community resources and community-based care. Discharge planners are therefore assuming a pivotal role in knowing what resources are available and linking patients with the most appropriate resource. With this increased emphasis on decreasing the length of stay, sometimes discharge planners may feel pressured to consider the hospital's interest before the patient's.[43] Certainly the role demands that although patient advocacy is inherent, one must also be a strong advocate for one's employer.

As more hospitals establish their own home care programs, equipment companies, and skilled nursing facilities, additional pressures may be placed on the discharge planner to make referrals to the hospital's programs in order to keep them viable. However, it is equally important that the discharge planner use these resources appropriately and guard the hospital against restraint of trade.[44] Devising specific written criteria as to which referrals are appropriate for the hospital's program will help to protect both the discharge planner and the hospital. Actively involving the patient and family in the selection of referral agencies, companies, or facilities will also help to avoid ethical and legal dilemmas. Careful documentation is then needed to verify that patients and families made an informed decision and that written criteria for the selection were indeed met.

Lawsuits against hospitals generally result from actual negligence or the patient's or family's perception that the hospital did not meet its duty.[45] Therefore, it is imperative that hospitals have written policies and procedures as well as documentation that hospital staff is following them. The policies and procedures are actually standards of care for discharge planning, and the discharge planning activities will be measured against these written policies. Periodic evaluation of the discharge planning program will identify gaps between written policy and actual practice. Once problems are identified there must be evidence that steps were taken to correct the discrepancy.

As pressures increase for discharge planners and they face ethical and legal questions with increasing frequency, they need to ask themselves the following questions:

- Can discharge planners identify patients who require their services without a specific order from a physician?
- Are there gaps between written policy and actual discharge planning practice?
- Can staff question an order or delay a discharge without recrimination?
- Does staff have access to legal counsel and administrative support?
- Are families given enough information regarding quality and cost of services to make an informed decision?

- Are patients and families knowingly referred to inappropriate resources?

The American Association for Continuity of Care (AACC) has developed a Code of Ethics and Standards for Hospital Continuity of Care (see Appendixes 5-A and 5-B). These are intended to serve as professional guides in helping discharge planners resolve some of the ethical and legal dilemmas facing them today.

NOTES

1. Joint Commission on Accreditation of Hospitals, *Accreditation Manual for Hospitals,* 1986 ed. (Chicago: JCAH, 1985).

2. M. LaMontagne and K. McKeehan, "Profile of a Continuing Care Program Emphasizing Discharge Planning," *Journal of Nursing Administration,* October 1975, p. 22.

3. E. Hartigan and D.J. Brown, *Discharge Planning for Continuity of Care,* Pub. No. 20-1977 (New York: National League for Nursing, 1985), p. 101.

4. American Nurses' Association, *Continuity of Care and Discharge Planning Programs in Institutions and Community Agencies,* Pub. Code NP-49, 3000 (Kansas City, Mo.: Author, 1975), p. 3.

5. K. Buckwalter, "Explaining the Process of Discharge Planning: Application to the Construct of Health," in *Continuity of Care: Advancing the Concept of Discharge Planning,* ed. E. McClelland, K. Kelly, and K. Buckwalter (Orlando, Fla.: Grune & Stratton, 1985), p. 6.

6. K. McKeehan, "Conceptual Framework for Discharge Planning," in *Continuing Care: A Multidisciplinary Approach to Discharge Planning,* ed. K. McKeehan (St. Louis: C. V. Mosby Co., 1981), pp. 3–4.

7. S. McCarthy, "Discharge Planning in a Primary Nursing System," *Discharge Planning Update* 4 (Fall 1983):10–14.

8. B. Leibowitz, "Impact of Intra-institutional Relocation," *Gerontologist* 14 (1974):293–95.

9. C.J. Coulton, R.E. Dunkle, R.A. Goode, and J. McIntosh, "Discharge Planning and Decision Making," *Health and Social Work* 7 (1982):253–61.

10. S. McCarthy, "Discharge Planning for the High Risk Infant," in *Home Care for the High Risk Infant,* ed. E. Ahmann. (Rockville, Md.: Aspen Publishers, 1986), p. 16.

11. H. Yura and M.B. Walsh, *The Nursing Process: Assessing, Planning, Implementing, Evaluating,* 3d ed. (New York: Appleton-Century-Crofts, 1978), p. 93.

12. B. Steffl and G. Eide, "Comprehensive Assessment: The Heart of Discharge Planning—A Nursing Perspective," *Discharge Planning Update* 1 (Winter 1981):3–5.

13. National League for Nursing Statement on Continuity of Nursing Care, August 1966.

14. Steffl and Eide, "A Nursing Perspective," pp. 3–5.

15. E. Bonander, "Comprehensive Assessment: The Heart of Discharge Planning—A Social Work Perspective," *Discharge Planning Update* 1 (Winter 1981):6–8.

16. C. Coulton, "Discharge Planning as a Decision Making Process," *Discharge Planning Update* 1 (Spring 1981):6–10.

17. S. McCarthy, "Discharge Planning in a Primary Nursing System," *Discharge Planning Update* 4 (Fall 1983):10–14.

18. Bonander, "A Social Work Perspective," pp. 6–8.

19. B. Sandvik, "Preadmission Screening: Key to Discharge Planning," *The Journal for Hospital Admitting Management* 3 (Winter 1985):16.

20. L. Cunningham, "Early Assessment for Discharge Planning," *Quality Review Bulletin* 7 (October 1981):11–16.

21. L. Rasmussen, "A Screening Tool Promotes Early Discharge Planning," *Nursing Management* 15 (May 1984):39–43.

22. McCarthy, "Discharge Planning for the High Risk Infant," p. 16.

23. J. Kitto and B. Dale, "Designing a Brief Discharge Planning Screen," *Nursing Management* 16 (September 1985):28–30.

24. C. Hollingsworth and B. Sokol, "Predischarge Family Conference," *JAMA* 239 (Feb. 20, 1978):740–41.

25. H.L. Van Hoozer, B.D. Bratton, P.M. Ostmoe, et al. *The Teaching Process, Theory and Practice in Nursing* (E. Norwalk, Conn.: Appleton-Century-Crofts, 1987).

26. Ibid.

27. Ibid.

28. C.C. Doak, L. Doak, J.H. Root, et al. *Teaching Patients with Low Literacy Skills* (Philadelphia: J.B. Lippincott Co., 1985).

29. Van Hoozer et al., *The Teaching Process.*

30. Doak et al., *Teaching Patients with Low Literacy Skills.*

31. B.K. Redman, *The Process of Patient Teaching in Nursing,* 5th ed. (St. Louis: C. V. Mosby Co., 1985).

32. Van Hoozer et al., *The Teaching Process.*

33. Ibid.

34. M.B. Hartsell and J.H. Ward, "Selecting Equipment Vendors for Children on Home Care," *MCN: The American Journal of Maternal Child Nursing* 10 (January/February 1985): 26–28.

35. J. Muenchow and B. Carlson, "Evaluating Programs of Discharge Planning," in *Continuity of Care: Advancing the Concept of Discharge Planning,* ed. E. McClelland, K. Kelly, and K. Buckwalter (Orlando, Fla.: Grune & Stratton, 1985), pp. 149–59.

36. S. Rossen, "Adapting Discharge Planning to Prospective Pricing," *Hospitals* 58 (March 1, 1984):71, 75, 79.

37. P. Roberts and T. Roberts, "Involvement in the Legislative Process: A Natural Step for Discharge Planners," *Discharge Planning Update* 4 (Winter 1984):5–9.

38. F.A. Wilson and D. Neuhauser, *Health Services in the United States,* 2d ed. (Cambridge, Mass.: Ballinger, 1985), p. 171.

39. M. Mundinger, *Home Care Controversy: Too Little, Too Late, Too Costly* (Rockville, Md.: Aspen Publishers, 1983).

40. F.J. Crittenden, *Discharge Planning for Health Care Facilities* (Los Angeles: University of California Extension Allied Health Publications, 1983).

41. J. George and E. Ahmann, "Community Resources for the Family of the High Risk

Infant," in E. Ahmann, ed., *Home Care of the High Risk Infant,* (Rockville, Md.: Aspen Publishers, 1986), p. 16.

42. F. Hoffman, "Diagnosis-related Groups: Fears and Realities," in *Continuity of Care: Advancing the Concept of Discharge Planning,* ed. E. McClelland, K. Kelly, and K. Buckwalter (Orlando, Fla.: Grune & Stratton, 1985), pp. 105–15.

43. R. Kane, "Discharge Planning and Multidisciplinary Teamwork: A Cautionary Note," *Discharge Planning Update* 2 (Winter 1982):9–13.

44. Discharge Planning Advisor, *Hospital Peer Review* 10 (Fall 1985):1–4.

45. Ibid.

Appendix 5-A

American Association for Continuity of Care
Standards for Hospital Continuity of Care*

Philosophy:

Continuity of care is an integral part of the healthcare delivery system which includes physicians' offices, clinics, HMOs, hospitals, home health agencies, extended care facilities and rehabilitation centers. The discharge planning process is an interdisciplinary approach that is centered on the patient and family or significant other to facilitate the transition of the patient from one level of care to another. It insures that preventive, therapeutic, rehabilitative and psycho/social, as well as medical needs, are included in the assessment, planning, implementation and evaluation process. Every patient benefits from and has the right to quality, coordinated continuity of care within available resources as an integral part of total patient care.

Principle:

Each hospital shall have in operation an organized continuing care program that assists with the provision of timely, achievable, quality discharge plans for patients utilizing available resources. The goals of the program shall be compatible with the goals of the hospital for high quality and effective patient care.

---

*Reprinted with permission of the American Association for Continuity of Care.

Standard I—Organization

There shall be evidence of a well-defined, organized interdisciplinary program designed to enhance continuity of care. Written policies and procedures that reflect optimal standards of practice shall guide the provision of continuity of care. The program shall be in accordance with the goals and objectives of the hospital.

Standard II—Discharge Planning Process

Discharge planning is an ongoing, interdisciplinary process. Each hospital department that has a direct effect on patient care shall enhance continuity of care through the appropriate utilization of hospital services, institutional facilities and community resources. The discharge planning process shall be integrated and coordinated by healthcare professionals.

Standard III—Patient/Family/Significant Other Participation

Patients and/or family and significant others shall be informed of and shall have access to healthcare professionals who will provide individualized, goal-directed discharge planning. Informed, patient-centered decision making is an essential component of the planning process.

Standard IV—Documentation

There shall be clear documentation of the discharge planning process in the patients' permanent medical records. Documentation is to include but not be limited to patients' continuing care needs and the discharge planning process.

Standard V—Review and Evaluation

There shall be mechanisms for the regular review and evaluation of the quality and appropriateness of continuing care practices and functions. Such mechanisms shall be designed to attain optimal achievable standards of continuity of care.

Standard VI—Professional Preparation

Continuing care professionals shall be prepared through appropriate education and orientation programs for their responsibilities in the provision of discharge planning. Healthcare professionals shall show continued efforts to maintain a high level of current knowledge in the field of continuity of care so as to meet both the patients' and hospital's needs within the healthcare delivery system.

Appendix 5-B

American Association for Continuity of Care
Code of Ethics*

In performing their relevant professional activities, all members of the American Association for Continuity of Care will:

1. Provide services to patients regardless of race, creed, color, age, or sexual preference.
2. Respect the patient's right to confidentiality, privacy and individuality.
3. Maintain professional integrity by neither seeking nor receiving personal compensation from a purveyor of services in return for the referral of a patient or patients to such purveyor.
4. Be responsible for informing the patient (or his/her representative) and the necessary medical and administrative personnel when continuity of care plan is judged inappropriate.
5. Maintain complete records, and appropriately document the continuity of care process including assessment, interventions and plan for implementation.
6. Promote interdisciplinary practice and interagency collaboration to achieve continuity of care.
7. Communicate an accurate assessment of patient care needs to service providers.
8. Accurately represent any known limitations of services.
9. Assure quality of practice through an ongoing evaluation process and participation in continuing education.

---

*Reprinted with permission of the American Association for Continuity of Care.

Chapter 6

Legal Aspects of Discharge Planning

Karen Arcidiacono*

---

*Ms. Arcidiacono is Associate Counsel for Greater Southeast Community Hospital, Washington, D.C.

6

Health care providers are developing delivery systems and practices in response to market forces and governmental reimbursement constraints. Although the potential liabilities of new ventures can be identified in general terms, the boundaries of those liabilities are often mere speculation. Discharge planning liabilities revolve around the practices of the individual health care professional, the policies of the facility or agency, and the interpretations of new legislation. Individuals providing care have to carefully juggle the patient's needs with the interests of the institution that employs them or extends them privileges to practice. This sets up ethical conflicts in addition to the potential legal dangers. Institutional providers seek to balance antitrust, professional liability (malpractice), profitability, and quality care concerns.

Much has been written about the impact of Medicare's prospective payment system (PPS) on the quality of care. A study reported by the House Select Committee on Aging found that Medicare patients are leaving hospitals sicker and are requiring more posthospital care since the implementation of PPS.[1] Discharge planners are recognizing this trend and are faced with a new legal risk perhaps best labeled "economic liability,"[2] in which patient injury results from premature hospital discharge. A recent case, *Wickline v. State of California*,[3] illustrates that the general area of economic liability was identifiable, but that the actual boundaries of risk are yet to be defined.

ECONOMIC LIABILITY

The *Wickline* case involved allegations that the employees of the state Medicaid program (Medi-Cal) negligently discontinued the patient's eli-

135

gibility for acute hospital care, causing premature hospital discharge. The program in place when treatment was initiated required preauthorization for treatment and approval for extensions in approved hospital stays. The surgical procedure to treat the plaintiff's right leg arteriosclerosis and occlusion was originally approved by Medi-Cal with a ten-day hospital stay. Over the course of the first five days of admission the plaintiff had a difficult postoperative course and had to be returned to surgery twice. Her physicians requested an eight-day extension for her hospital stay. The extension was not approved by the Medi-Cal reviewing nurse. Instead the reviewing nurse referred the case to a physician consultant. Medi-Cal protocol gave the nurse reviewer the authority to approve requests as submitted, while permitting only a physician consultant to deny the request outright or authorize fewer days than requested. Without independent inquiry into the patient's case, the physician consultant approved a four-day extension based on a conversation with the nurse reviewer. The plaintiff was discharged at the end of the four days without further attempts by her physicians to secure another extension. The surgeon testified that his decision not to seek a further extension was influenced by his impression that Medi-Cal's physician consultant had the state's interest in mind more than the patient's welfare.[4] The surgeon gave the discharge order, but nine days after discharge the plaintiff was readmitted with complications to her right leg. She had been experiencing pain and color changes for a few days before readmission. Over the next three weeks the plaintiff underwent a below-the-knee amputation, and when her condition did not resolve she underwent a further above-the-knee amputation.

The court held that Medi-Cal was not liable, since it is the attending physician's responsibility to decide when and whether to discharge a patient. The court went on to state that

> third party payors of health care services can be held legally accountable when medically inappropriate decisions result from defects in the design or implementation of cost containment mechanisms. . . . However, the physician who complies without protest with the limitations imposed by a third party payor, when his medical judgment dictates otherwise, cannot avoid his ultimate responsibility for his patient's care.[5]

Wickline is the first case decided under California law in which the plaintiff sought to tie the health care payer into the medical malpractice causation chain. It is certainly just the beginning of this new line of cases. Because *Wickline* is still in the appeal process, it will take time before we have a reading on how courts will handle situations in which treatment decisions are made in response to utilization review procedures dictated by third party payers.

New federal regulations have been adopted to require hospitals to inform Medicare patients of their right to challenge discharge and the method they must use to formally institute a challenge.[6] Beginning in March of 1986 hospitals faced administrative and judicial penalties, including possible revocation of licensure, unless they provided Medicare patients with a notice explaining the discharge appeal process by peer review organizations (PROs) and encouraging patients to ask questions of their doctors. The notice was developed by national health care organizations, including the American Hospital Association, in response to an initial draft by the Health Care Financing Administration. "An Important Message from Medicare" uses bold lettering to emphasize that the patient's discharge date should be determined solely by medical needs, not by "DRGs" (diagnosis-related groups). The regulations provide that once the appeal is initiated, the PRO must render a decision in three working days. If the PRO judges the discharge appropriate, the patient does not become accountable for charges until the fourth calendar day after the hospital gave notice of discharge. If the discharge is inappropriate, the patient is allowed to remain in the hospital and the facility is liable for all costs.

Regulations like the one just described cause ethical dilemmas for health care providers. As health care consumers in the United States, we have all come to expect that every person will receive the best care available regardless of ability to pay. As health care professionals, we know the economic realities. A nondiscriminatory method of providing care is indeed expensive; without safeguards it may break down into a two-tier system based on the ability to guarantee payment.

Hospitals are conscious of the need to increase efficiency and may consider using financial and length of stay statistics as part of the medical staff reappointment process. Thus a physician who "costs" a hospital more to treat patients than reimbursement covers may have his or her privileges reduced unless he or she is able to justify patient needs in terms of severity or acuity of illness. Alterations in practice patterns may potentially improve or worsen the quality of patient care. Curtailing unnecessary diagnostic or therapeutic procedures should decrease morbidity and mortality. On the other hand, if needed services are curtailed, the quality of patient care will be adversely affected.[7]

STANDARDS OF CARE

Often referred to as negligence, professional liability is a form of tort law in which four basic elements of the case must be proved by the plaintiff. Briefly, the plaintiff must show that the health care provider owed a *duty* to render care, that the duty was breached, and that the *breach* was the *cause* of an identifiable *injury*. The elements of a tort action are not subject to change; however, the standard of care (which defines whether a breach has occurred) will change as new technologies are developed and health care delivery models evolve. In the *Wickline* case, the experts testifying at trial opined that the physicians acted within the prevailing standard of care.[8] Note that the plaintiff's surgery took place in 1977. Experts reviewing the medical records under 1987 standards might draw a different conclusion.

Standards are set in a variety of ways. Most often they are defined in written guidelines of a recognized professional organization, or in the stated policies and procedures of the facility rendering care. The standard of care is also evidenced by the practice in the community. To adduce the standard of care in a patient setting, it is best to follow the "reasonable man" test; that is, determine what a resonable practitioner with similar background and experience would do under like circumstances.[9]

Scanning the health care literature, many standards are advocated for good patient care. One recently published study[10] places highest priority on the physician-patient interaction component of patient involvement in health care because "it is there that patients can have the greatest impact on medical decisions and the course of treatment." Likewise, nursing journals may advocate an equally high standard: "Where once patients depended upon their physicians for teaching relative to health problems, this function has been transferred largely into the nursing area."[11] In the area of discharge planning, liability may attach to every health care discipline that interacts with the patient. Social workers, too, have published guidelines or recommendations regarding the role of the social worker in discharge planning.[12]

Published standards, like internal policies and procedures, are necessary evils in health care administration. They set the ground rules for practice, encourage consistent quality care, and act as training tools for new staff members. At the same time they become powerful weapons in the hands of plaintiff's counsel when a standard or policy has been violated. Those who delineate professional responsibilities in the form of guidelines or policies need to keep two goals in mind: providing the patient with the best care available and setting performance standards realistically. Lawsuits are often the result of frustrated expectations, whether or not the expectation is attainable[13]. As the quality of medical care continues to improve in this country, expectations also rise. One very plausible reason for the increased number of lawsuits facing practitioners and facilities is that when expectations are disappointed, disappointment turns into anger. This is not to say that we, as health care providers, should lower the standards we set for our disciplines. We must continue to strive for high-quality health care, mindful that setting unattainable standards will make for legal headaches later.

As discussed in earlier chapters of this book, the National League for Nursing published a statement on continuity of nursing care in 1966.[14] The Steering Committee that developed this statement made strong recommendations that were clearly ahead of their time. More than 20 years later the recommendations of the National League for Nursing are not yet uniformly adopted or implemented throughout the United States.

THEORIES OF LIABILITY AND SUGGESTIONS FOR DEFENSE

In addition to economic liability there are many other types of negligence claims.[15] The claims that immediately come to mind involve informed consent, patient abandonment, negligent selection or monitoring of personnel, and equipment or product failure.

Patient Information and Education

Claims of abandonment and lack of informed consent should be inversely related to the quality and quantity of patient interaction and education about the treatment regimen itself and the limitations to treatment. The best defense to these claims is often the one little noticed: strong rapport between patient and provider. The second best defense is thorough documentation of the care given and efforts undertaken. Defense of potential lawsuits should not be the sole motivating factor behind a well-orchestrated discharge planning system that fosters strong patient relations and requires good documentation. The motivating factor must always be quality patient care. Two of the changes predicted as a result of PPS are an increased need for patient teaching and expanded long-term and home health care services.[16] If practitioners can take the time to talk to, listen to, and express concern for their patients, they will be simultaneously protecting themselves and helping those whom they are committed to help.[17]

Informed consent is much more than the signature on a document labeled "Authorization" or "Release." It is the exchange between practitioner and patient that imparts enough information regarding risks, benefits, and alternatives to the treatment proposed to allow the patient to make a reasoned decision. Every adult of sound mind has a legal right to determine what will be done to his or her body.[18] This right to make health care decisions extends into the situation where a patient or family rejects options that the practitioner finds to be in the patient's best interest. It may be a patient's adamant refusal of nursing home placement or refusal to learn injection techniques necessary for continued well-being.[19]

Informed consent can be documented in a variety of ways. The most common is the consent form used for experimental and invasive diagnostic or therapeutic procedures. Tailored checklists or instruction sheets can be helpful tools evidencing informed consent. For example, a checklist indicating the dates when a home dialysis or hyperalimentation patient first demonstrated proficiency in each specific task necessary to prepare, use, and disassemble equipment is invaluable. Discharge instruction sheets developed for specific conditions and used particularly by emergency or outpatient surgical departments have the added benefit that a signed copy can be kept in the patient's medical record and a duplicate copy can be sent home with the patient or responsible party. Obtaining a signature to indicate receipt of information seems to reinforce the importance of that information. The Middletown Psychiatric Center, part of the New York State public mental health system, uses a discharge planning form[20] with a signature line under the following statement:

STATEMENTS OF PARTICIPATION IN PLANNING PROCESS:

I have participated in the development of this plan. I am aware of the plan and it meets with my approval.

Another method that documents the patient's training and ability to perform necessary techniques, such as self-administration of medication, uses behavioral progress notes to indicate that the patient has demonstrated a proper technique or knowledge.[21]

For routine discharge planning, standardized forms may be adequate. More difficult situations—for example, patient or family members who frustrate discharge planning by missing appointments or failing to follow the treatment regimen after ample instructions are given—require more detailed documentation of plans and efforts undertaken by practitioners. This is particularly critical when a patient or family feels helpless because of a lack of suitable options. The discharge planner needs to be aware of, to identify for patient recognition, and to document gaps in community services when there are no available services to meet the patient's post-hospital needs.[22] There will always be cases in which a "perfect fit" for patient needs and available services cannot be made. Although it is frustrating for patient and practitioner, both parties must accept the best the situation can offer. Not having adequate options available is a very different situation from, and cannot be confused with, releasing a patient to an inappropriate level of care in response to institutional or third party payer pressures. The latter situation is closely aligned with patient abandonment.

Abandonment claims arise in situations other than release from acute care facilities. Home health agencies face these potential claims if the patient becomes noncompliant with instructions, the home environment becomes unsafe for patient and practitioner, or the patient becomes ineligible for reimbursement benefits. There is no clear-cut method to handle such situations without incurring liability. The hallmarks of a properly managed situation include allowing adequate time to make alternative arrangements, providing written notice of the intention to terminate the home care relationship and a list of alternative community services, and providing all necessary information so that the next caregiver can smoothly assume the patient care regimen.

Probably the most difficult case to deal with in an acute care facility is one in which the patient is incompetent and the family, for whatever reason, refuses to cooperate in the hospital's discharge planning efforts. A family's refusal to provide financial information to secure nursing home placement is unfortunately becoming a recurrent problem. Because the problem is so difficult, the methods to resolve it must be creative and they may appear to be drastic. Some states have "destitute parent" statutes that place a legal duty (over the moral duty) to care for an infirm parent.[23] In jurisdictions in which no statutory family duty is defined, a hospital may need to give the family written notice of intention to petition the court for guardianship or conservatorship and, if the family refuses to cooperate after such notice, may need to file the necessary petitions and affidavits in court. Legal proceedings may also be warranted if a competent patient who has no known family or responsible party becomes incompetent later in the admission, leaving no one to give consent for necessary medical procedures or nursing home placement.

Corporate Liability

Corporate liability may take the form of negligent selection or monitoring of staff or independent contractors and of liability for defective products or devices. Hospitals are well aware of potential liability for negligent credentialing in the context of granting clinical privileges to physicians, dentists, and allied health care practitioners.[24] This is an area that may expand, since patients are often discharged to the care of home health agencies that depend on independent contractors to supply such services as physical therapy, respiratory therapy, or equipment installation or service. This area is beyond the scope of this chapter; however, discharge planners must know the capabilities and limitations of the referred agencies and document any inquiries made or actions taken, including informing patients and families.[25]

Product liability is yet another area for hospital liability concerns. Patients who are discharged with indwelling catheters, feeding tubes, portable oxygen, intravenous infusion pumps, and like technologies may look to the hospital if the equipment or device fails. Hospitals cannot assume that if a piece of equipment fails, the manufacturer will be liable.[26] This is especially true if hospital personnel gave instructions for product use or maintenance or fitted the device. Again, the hospital that sends the patient home with equipment must make inquiries into who is responsible to warranty the fitness for a particular use, must train the patient or family adequately, and must document the training and follow-up actions taken.

Other Lawsuit Defenses

Three defenses available to the practitioner have already been discussed:

1. Give the best care available, according to the standards of the discipline.
2. Accurately and legibly document the care given.
3. Be diligent in keeping good rapport with the patient and family.

Risk management and quality assurance are two other noteworthy defenses available to the administrator of the facility or agency. Concurrent and retrospective screening mechanisms, along with occurrence reporting, have the same roles in discharge planning as they have in evaluations of medical and nursing care in acute hospitalizations.

Risk management screens should be set up to identify at least the following:

- unclear intake/referral/feedback criteria
- untimely or delayed discharge planning activity
- improper utilization or malfunction of equipment
- potential for inadequate or unsafe vendor services
- improperly trained staff
- use of lower-level staff to give high-technology care
- inadequate insurance coverage for independent contractors
- inadequate communication with referring physician.

In addition to these screens, risk management efforts should encourage yearly policy review and revision. Review of forms used for patient teaching should be ongoing in at least a random fashion to ensure that staff members are supplying the necessary documentation and that the form is adequate and current.

Quality assurance screening may incorporate some of the criteria identified for risk management but should also focus on the trends that cause inpatient or emergency admission within a short time of hospital discharge (15 days may be the appropriate time frame). Reasons that often cause readmission are:

- patients leaving against medical advice
- patient noncompliance with instructions
- inadequate instructions
- discharge to an inappropriate level of care
- an unrelated medical problem
- unanticipated complications not present on discharge
- premature discharge
- transfer to another facility before stabilization.

Quality assurance activities may also use telephone follow-up or patient questionnaires to identify problems. Some hospitals have even set up telephone hot lines, having the dual purposes of monitoring for inappropriate discharges or referrals and marketing to promote good relations with patients.[27]

ANTITRUST CONCERNS

There are three ways that an acute care facility discharging to home health agencies (or long-term facilities) can come under attack of the antitrust laws, more specifically the Sherman Antitrust Act.[28] Section 1 of the Act prohibits restraint of trade in the form of *tying arrangements,* in which the hospital owns or controls the agency to which it refers patients, or *exclusive dealings* with an agency without hospital ownership or control. Section 2 of the Act prohibits conspiracies or attempts to monopolize and monopolization.

Because of the rapid expansion in the hospital-sponsored segment of the home health market—a growth of 133 percent in Medicare-certified hospital home care programs between December 1983 and August 1986[29]— a detailed discussion of tying arrangements would seem the most relevant for hospital providers who either have just entered the home care market or are considering adding the service.

For many years the courts were reluctant to apply the antitrust laws to the health care field because of the belief that health care professions were exempt from coverage. That perception has changed radically in recent years, most notably in the *Hyde*[30] case decided by the Supreme Court in 1984. *Hyde* caused the Court to examine an exclusive contract in which one group of physicians supplied all anesthesiology services within a given hospital. The anesthesiologist who was denied privileges because of the exclusive contract brought the antitrust action, charging that the hospital had "tied" the use of operating suites with anesthesia services. Tying arrangements are agreements to sell one product (here, the use of operating rooms) but only on the condition that the buyer also purchase the tied product (here, anesthesia services).[31] The full Court agreed that the particular contract between the hospital and the anesthesia group giving rise to this controversy did not violate antitrust laws. The Court was divided on the legal analysis to be used in tying cases. The majority focused on two issues: whether the hospital and anesthesia services were separate products and whether the hospital possessed sufficient market power to force patients to buy services they would not otherwise have purchased. The majority found that the hospital and anesthesia services were separate products because separate markets for the services existed, as evidenced by billing procedures and requests of patients or surgeons for a particular anesthesiologist. Once the Court had determined that the separate services had been tied, it looked to the hospital's market power (its ability to force patients to buy services they would not otherwise purchase), noting that refusal to sell the services separately is not "per se" illegal.[32] The legal reasoning of the majority continued after finding "per se" condemnation inappropriate by finding no hospital antitrust liability for unreasonably restraining competition, noting that there had been no showing that the market as a whole had been affected by the contract.[33]

The legal reasoning advocated by concurring justices would require the existence of separate products; however, it would not apply a "separate market" test. It would instead look to the economic determination of whether the tying of products is beneficial and whether there is a substantial threat that the seller will acquire market power.[34]

The legal significance of *Hyde* has applicability to both hospital-sponsored and independent home care agencies that receive patients from a single referral source. The significance is that future controversies in these areas will probably be decided by a rule of reason standard, the ultimate issue being whether the arrangement unreasonably restrains competition. A court will first look at whether patients are *required* as a precondition to hospital care to use the affiliated home care agency. To explore this issue, a court would look at whether discharge planners are instructed to refer to any agency with an appropriate level of services to meet the patient's needs, whether policies permit discharge planners to refer to nonaffiliated agencies, whether such referrals are actually made in practice, and whether the home health agency recruits or accepts referrals from facilities other than its affiliate. The court will also examine the hospital's economic interest in the home care agency.

To date, no court has addressed a tying arrangement between hospital and home care agency or long-term facility. There is also no absolute way to predict what will trigger antitrust liability under Section 1 of the Sherman Act, since the hospital's market power is determined by the geographic area that is considered the "relevant" market. The smaller the "relevant" market, the stronger the hospital's power will appear. The converse is also true. In the *Hyde* case, for example, the Supreme Court disagreed with the lower court's narrow definition of geographic market (the East Bank of Jefferson Parish), adopting instead a larger market encompassing all of metropolitan New Orleans.

Section 2 of the Sherman Act focuses on monopolies and attempts to monopolize. The monopolization theory may come into play if the hospital is a competitor in the home health market and it possesses sufficient market power over referrals, that is, a large percentage of patients who need home health services are discharged from that hospital. Although not concretely stated in the law, 60 percent is a rough estimate of where liability may begin.[35] Even without sufficient market power a hospital may be subject to an "attempted monopolization" claim if it refuses to make referrals to another home health agency simply because of the competition and not because of the quality or quantity of services offered by the competitor. Again, a court would examine the stated policy of the hospital regarding patient referral for posthospital care as well as the actual practices of the discharge planners.

Administrators and discharge planners need to guard against inappropriate discharges to a single facility or agency for both quality care concerns and restraint of trade concerns, yet the advantages of developing strong links between acute care and long-term facilities or home health agencies cannot be overlooked. Strong links have positive outcomes on both financial and patient care fronts.[36]

ANTIFRAUD AND ABUSE AMENDMENTS

In 1977 Congress enacted the Medicare-Medicaid Antifraud and Abuse Amendments.[37] The intent of the amendments was to eliminate double billing practices and provider kickbacks. Although few cases have been brought under the antifraud amendments, there are several situations that may cause the hospital to incur liability. The factual situation here that may trigger liability may be quite similar to the facts surrounding an exclusive dealing antitrust matter, in which a hospital has either a formal or an informal agreement with a particular home care agency and consistently refers all or most of its patients to that home care agency.

In one recent case, *U.S. v. Greber*,[38] a physician who received fees in connection with tests performed by a laboratory was found to violate the antifraud statute. The payments by the laboratory were illegal, since they were intended to induce the physician to use the laboratory services even though the payments were also intended to compensate for professional services.[39]

In an article discussing the activities that may trigger the antifraud and antiabuse provisions,[40] the following situations were identified as potentially problematic, thus requiring special attention:

- joint venture, in which the home health agency incurs little financial risk and supplies little capital or services
- an agreement linking rate of return to number of patient referrals
- an agreement in which the home health agency secures valuable materials, equipment, or services at a substantially reduced rate.

CONCLUSION

The purpose of this chapter is to highlight those legal dangers that have recently emerged in discharge planning as well as those theories of liability that have not been tested in court but are predicted. The corporation primarily faces liability on two levels: tort and antitrust. The individual caregiver also faces tort issues, but they may be more intense, since ethical issues compound the complexity of treatment decisions. The administrator of a discharge planning program needs to continually assess the potential liabilities in view of new services offered and new statutory or judicial standards.

NOTES

1. Sustaining Quality Health Care Under Cost Containment, Report at the Joint Hearing Before the Select Committee on Aging and the Task Force on Rural Health, U.S. House of Rep. (Feb. 2, 1985) (P.L. 99-499).

2. Burda, *Lawyers Ponder New Sources of Liability Suits,* 60 HOSPITALS, Aug. 5, 1986, at 28.

3. 228 Cal. Rptr. 661 (1986).

4. *Id.* at 667.

5. *Id.* at 671.

6. 42 C.F.R. § 466.78(b)(3) (1986).

7. Mushlin, *The Analysis of Clinical Practices: Shedding Light on Cost Containment Opportunities in Medicine,* 11 QUALITY REV. BULL., Dec. 1985, at 378.

8. *Wickline,* 228 Cal. Rptr. at 667.

9. For a discussion of physician responsibilities in home care, *see* Borders, *Reducing Liability Risk in Home Care,* 20 PATIENT CARE, Mar. 15, 1986, at 57.

10. Greenfield, Kapland, & Ware, *Expanding Patient Involvement in Patient Care,* 102 ANN. INT. MED., Apr. 1985, at 520.

11. Creighton, *Law for the Nurse Manager,* 16 NURSING, Jan. 1985, at 12.

12. AHA, Society for Hosp. Social Work Directors of the Am. Hosp. Ass'n, THE ROLE OF THE SOCIAL WORKER IN DISCHARGE PLANNING (Position Statement) (1985) [hereinafter Position Statement].

13. AHA, MEDICAL MALPRACTICE TASK FORCE REPORT ON TORT REFORM (1985).

14. *See* Chapter 5, The Process of Discharge Planning, at 107, *see also* Chapter 1, An Overview of Discharge Planning, at 7.

15. *See generally Discharge Planners' Actions Reduce Legal Vulnerability,* 10 DISCHARGE PLANNING ADVISOR HOSP. PEER REV., Fall 1985, at 1.

16. F.M. Hoffman, *Diagnosis-Related Groups: Fears and Realities,* in CONTINUITY OF CARE: ADVANCING THE CONCEPT OF DISCHARGE PLANNING 105 (1985).

17. Brenner & Gerken, *Informed Consent: Myths and Risk Management Alternatives,* 12 QUALITY REV. BULL., Dec. 1986, at 420.

18. Schloendorff v. Society of New York Hospitals, 211 N.Y. 125, 105 N.E. 92 (1914).

19. *See generally* President's Commission for the Study of Ethical Problems in Medicine and Biomedical and Behavioral Research, MAKING HEALTH CARE DECISIONS: THE ETHICAL AND LEGAL IMPLICATIONS OF INFORMED CONSENT IN THE PATIENT-PRACTITIONER RELATIONSHIP (1982); AHA, THE HOSPITAL'S RESPONSIBILITY FOR PATIENT EDUCATION SERVICES (1981).

20. Individual Service Plan, State of New York, Office of Mental Health Form OMH-6 in O'Sullivan & Brody, *Discharge Planning for the Mentally Disabled,* 12 QUALITY REV. BULL., Feb. 1986, at 55, 64.

21. For a discussion of progress note documentation in terms of behaviors successfully demonstrated by the patient before discharge, *see* Chapter 1, An Overview of Discharge Planning at 13.

22. Position Statement, *supra* note 12.

23. *See* MD. FAM. LAW CODE ANN. §§13-101(c), 13-102(a) (1986) (adult child who has sufficient means may not neglect or refuse to provide food, shelter, care, and clothing for a parent who has no means of subsistence and cannot be self-supporting because of old age, or mental or physical infirmity).

24. *See* Darling v. Charleston Community Memorial Hosp., 33 Ill. 2d 326, 211 N.E.2d 253 (1965), *cert. denied,* 383 U.S. 946 (1966) (suggesting that hospital governing body has a duty to establish mechanisms to evaluate quality of patient care provided by hospital and medical staff and, where necessary, to take action to avoid unreasonable risk of harm to patients arising from treatment provided by a nonemployed attending physician); Gonzalez v. Nork and Mercy Hosp., 143 Cal. Rptr. 240 (Sup. Ct. 1978) (specifying hospital duty to create a mechanism by which it may discover staff member inadequacies and duty to act to prevent patient harm when poor performance is discovered); Johnson v. Misericordia Community Hosp., 301 N.W.2d 156 (1981) (finding hospital duty to properly review a physician's credentials).

25. For a more detailed discussion of liability for monitoring staff and independent contractors, *see* Tehan & Colegrove, *Risk Management and Home Health Care: The Time is Now,* 12 QUALITY REV. BULL., May 1986, at 179.

26. Burda, *Five Future Areas of Liability Risks Haunt Providers,* 60 HOSPITALS, Nov. 1986, at 48.

27. Giloth, *Incentives for Planned Patient Education,* 11 QUALITY REV. BULL., Oct. 1985, at 295.

28. 15 U.S.C. §§1–7 (1982).

29. *See* Burda, *supra* note 26.

30. Jefferson Parish Hosp. District No. 2 v. Hyde, 104 S. Ct. 1551 (1984).

31. Northern Pac. Ry. v. United States, 356 U.S. 1, 5 (1958).

32. *Hyde,* 104 S. Ct. at 1558.

33. *Id.* at 1568.

34. Miriani, Jefferson Parish Hospital v. Hyde: *Antitrust Tying Arrangements,* 59 TUL. L. REV. 1591 (1985).

35. Philp, *Home-Health Referrals: Some Legal Guidelines,* 59 HOSPITALS, Dec. 1, 1985, at 72.

36. Katz, *QA Update: Developing Hospital and Nursing Home Links,* 11 QUALITY REV. BULL., Oct. 1985, at 313.

37. 42 U.S.C. §1395nn (1982).

38. 760 F.2d 68 (3d Cir. 1985).

39. *Id.* at 72.

40. Randall, *Charting a Course Through the Gray of Criminal Charges of Fraud and Abuse,* 4 CARING, June 1985, at 28, 29.

Future Issues

Developing Discharge Planning Programs: Current and Future Models and Strategies

Patricia A. O'Hare

7

Discharge planning is necessary at all levels of care. Part III presents innovative models and strategies for discharge planning and continuity of care planning from acute care, the nursing home, the home health agency, the physician's office, the health maintenance organization (HMO), and the workplace. In this first chapter there is a brief discussion of discharge planning from the acute care setting with specific strategies presented for your consideration.

DISCHARGE PLANNING FROM ACUTE CARE

The acute care hospital is changing. Acuity levels of patients are rising and the care is becoming more complex. Joint ventures and diversification have broadened the hospital's base. Hospitals are beginning to operate on a continuing care model rather than exclusively on an acute care model. The establishment of the linkages within health care is critical for the necessary services and resources to be developed. It is essential that discharge planners be actively involved in identifying the need for and participating in the development of community services and resources. Community alternative services such as adult day care, sheltered housing, and case management can reduce the need for hospitalization and institutionalization. Discharge planners need to know what alternative modes of care are available, as well as how effective they are, and then appropriately use them.

Continuity of care "must be the backbone of any health care delivery system designed to meet the needs of the American people" and "can best be achieved when the focus is on the patient and his family."[1]

. . . staff boundary-spanning roles linking the hospital with other community health and welfare agencies become of crucial importance. Without effective human links to form the interorganizational bridges there cannot be the flow of patients, communication, resources, and joint interagency activities necessary for the provision of comprehensive services.

Systematic preadmission coordination is essential. Discharge planning for continuity of care must be initiated with the client's first contact with the health care system. Preadmission planning from the physician's office, as discussed by O'Brien in Chapter 10, includes assessment, teaching, referrals to other agencies, and involvement of community agencies before an admission. Preadmission planning by the hospital could also include these components.

Once the person is hospitalized, monitoring by the utilization review department assures that discharge planning is instituted in the acute care setting. The multidisciplinary focus of discharge planning is readily apparent. Hospitals are moving away from the discharge planning nurse and discharge planning social worker being based in separate departments. Instead, professionals from both disciplines may be located in the quality assurance or risk management department. Still another model might include the admissions department, business office, quality assurance department, discharge planning or continuing care department all under the same administrator. In this way, admissions, discharges, and quality within the organization are administratively under the control of one manager.

The discharge planning program is able to monitor admissions and discharges from the hospital as well as provide case management of the patients while they are hospitalized. There can be cost-efficiency through comprehensive assessment, beginning at the earliest possible point and with case management as part of the discharge planning process.

For comprehensive assessments and referrals to take place there must be ". . . a comprehensive assessment tool and a mechanism for translating assessment information into presumptive service needs."[3] According to the Long-Term Care Information System (LTCIS) developed by Falcone, specific assessment items are used to predict a person's need for different types of service. For example, dependence in five of seven activities of daily living is used to predict that nursing service of some kind will be needed for that person.[4] There are actually two levels of prediction; one is the presumptive need for a type of service and the other suggests the highest level of skill or intensity of service required.[5] The Omnibus Budget Reconciliation Act of 1986 has charged the Secretary of Health and Human

Services with the development of a "Uniform Needs Assessment Instrument" that

(A) evaluates
 (i) the functional capacity of an individual,
 (ii) the nursing and other care requirements of the individual to meet health care needs and to assist with functional incapacities, and
 (iii) the social and familial resources available to the individual to meet those requirements; and
(B) can be used by discharge planners, hospitals, nursing facilities, other health care providers, and fiscal intermediaries in evaluating an individual's need for post-hospital extended care services, home health services, and long-term care services of a health-related or supportive nature.[6]

It further states that "The Secretary shall report to Congress, not later than January 1, 1989, on the instrument or instruments developed under this section."[7] It was also specified that the instrument(s) will be developed

> . . . in consultation with an advisory panel, appointed by the Secretary, that includes experts in the delivery of post-hospital extended care services, home health services, and long-term care services and includes representatives of hospitals, of physicians, of skilled nursing facilities, of home health agencies, of long-term care providers, of fiscal intermediaries, and of medicare beneficiaries.

Will this "Uniform Needs Assessment Instrument" be useful in furthering the comprehensive assessment and referral systems that are needed for ongoing care? Certainly uniformity and consistency of data collection instruments will help. However, what is crucial is how this information is used by the community of providers to arrange and facilitate ongoing services. Also essential will be changes in reimbursement favoring post-hospital and long-term care in a variety of settings.

Evaluation of the process and outcomes of discharge planning in acute care is also needed. The discharge planning process can be audited concurrently and retrospectively, using criteria such as appropriateness, timeliness, effectiveness, collaborative process, and documentation.[9] These criteria must be defined in measurable terms. For example, timeliness might be operationally defined as the initial discharge planning assessment being recorded in the patient's chart within 48 hours of admission. The data obtained through the concurrent and retrospective audits will assist the health care professionals in improving discharge planning within the hospital.

In looking further at discharge planning in acute care, the rounds that are frequently mentioned in the literature as an integral part of the process need to be given greater consideration. These weekly rounds, whether called discharge planning rounds or patient care rounds, are a mechanism for casefinding and assessment. They provide an opportunity for early and continuous assessment. They also provide the occasion for a determination of who does not require discharge planning. To be effective, goals are needed for the rounds. An example of goals developed and used can be seen in Exhibits 7-1 and 7-2. The Interdisciplinary Continuity of Care Rounds (Exhibit 7-1) were conducted on the patient care units, with the time selected for the meeting depending on the unit nursing staff.

Because it was not possible for the rehabilitation therapists to schedule themselves for all of these rounds, the discharge planning rounds (Exhibit

Exhibit 7-1 Interdisciplinary Continuity of Care Rounds

Interdisciplinary Continuity of Care Rounds are held weekly on the medical, surgical units (see Goals).

Participants:
  Nursing, Social Service, Dietary, Representative from Pastoral Care, Utilization Review Coordinator.

Goals (Broad Statements):
1. *Foster* interdisciplinary *communication.*
2. *Identify patient care needs*—both in hospital and long-term needs, e.g., need to know more about home situation—where patients come from, who is available to help at discharge, etc.; patient teaching with family/significant other included in teaching; what supplies/equipment needed at home, etc.
3. *Opportunity for interdisciplinary education.* As health care providers we need to know what is available in the community, not only service agencies, but also self-help groups. Need to think of the total person and effects illness/health problem has on him/her as a person, as a member of a family, as a member of a community. There is a need to know "Where to Turn" and when to refer to another discipline or agency. Effective interdisciplinary continuity of care planning always considers the patient/family as members of the health team.
4. *Identify potential discharge problems* for referral to appropriate discipline or agency for assessment and follow-up. No referrals will be acted upon without consultation with the physician.
5. *Avoid fragmentation of services.*

Exhibit 7-2 Discharge Planning Rounds

Discharge Planning Rounds (Nursing, Physical Therapy, Occupational Therapy, Social Service) will be held every Wednesday from 8–9 A.M. in the ground floor Conference Room.

Goals:
1. Identify potential discharge problems and refer to appropriate discipline for assessment—follow-up.
2. Plan for providing continued services at the appropriate level of care after discharge from the acute care facility.
3. Foster interdisciplinary communication, coordination, and colleague support.
4. Provide an opportunity for interdisciplinary education.

7-2) were held weekly in a conference room in or near the physical therapy department. At these rounds, patients from any patient care unit could be scheduled for discussion, and the various disciplines, including the nurse from the unit, actively participated. Occasionally the medical, surgical, or orthopedic resident would attend the discharge planning rounds. These rounds provided a forum for interdisciplinary communication, coordination, and colleague support. All disciplines had input into developing the goals for the rounds. Goals help to clarify the purpose of the rounds and play a basic role in their overall organization.

The time in rounds and the size of the rounds team are two additional areas for consideration. In a pre-PPS research study, "Examining the Discharge Planning Process: An Evaluation of Two Models in an Acute Care Community Hospital," O'Hare[10] measured the average time spent in rounds to review 27 to 30 patients. The average time ranged from 48.5 minutes for the three-provider model to 54.5 minutes for the six-provider model. The three-provider model consisted of the nurse on the unit, the social worker, and the discharge planning nurse coordinator. The six-provider model was the nurse on the unit, the social worker, the discharge planning nurse coordinator, the health promotion coordinator, the dietitian, and the representative from the pastoral care department. The six-provider group probed for and identified more needs at the rounds, but they followed through less thoroughly than the three-provider group. Planning differences were noted not only between the two groups, but also within the groups, depending on whether or not patients were discussed at rounds only one time or multiple times. The rounds are part of the discharge planning process that warrant further investigation. For some participants they may be viewed as nonessential and as too time-consuming for what they yield. Documentation of what information the rounds actually contribute to the discharge planning process is important. In this way it can be assessed whether or not rounds are an efficient and effective manner of obtaining information and what goal(s) are being met by using this forum for interdisciplinary interaction.

Measuring discharge planning from an outcome perspective is also essential. Reviewing patients' charts to ascertain whether or not those who were to be referred to agencies in the community were indeed referred is an example of an outcome evaluation. If a patient was not referred to the community agency, is the reason for the nonreferral documented? If the patient was referred, then the next step is to ascertain if the requested services were provided. Lindenberg and Coulton, in their study "Planning for Posthospital Care: A Follow-up Study," found that "for most categories with services planned, only 65 to 75 percent of the patients received adequate services one month after discharge."[11] The adequacy of services was based on social workers' and patients' ratings of services. These data are required so that the appropriateness and effectiveness of the discharge plan and community resources can be evaluated. Outcomes of discharge planning from acute care need greater emphasis and development.

Another area to consider is what is termed "preventive discharge planning" by Dintenfass and Winter.[12] Preventive discharge planning is long-range planning for the patient who may be diagnosed in the physician's office or a clinic as having a neuropsychiatric disorder that will affect his or her mental capacity and competency in the future. This patient and family might be referred to the social worker in the acute care setting, unless a system exists in the physician's office, such as described by O'Brien in Chapter 10, or in the community. The discharge planning team would:

- educate the patient and family regarding the diagnosis and ongoing care management;
- identify support groups and assist with referrals to them;
- assist with referrals, as indicated, to agencies providing such services as homemaker, personal care, transportation, and respite care;
- assist with referrals to legal counsel regarding power of attorney or guardianship;
- maintain periodic contact with patient and family to reassess needs; and
- maintain periodic contact with the physician or clinic to keep them apprised of changes in the patient's status.[13]

The implementation of preventive discharge planning makes good sense. It would require communication and coordination on the part of all health professionals involved, but it is one example of the essential linkages that are needed in the health care delivery system today. These linkages will be even more critical as the population ages.

Another area in which creative approaches for linkages would be required is when working with people with limited options. As discussed in Chapter 5, a thorough assessment of the patient and his or her situation is essential. When working with the indigent population, an understanding of how the patient has survived to this point is essential. This includes understanding the home situation and social supports or, in the case of the homeless, determining the shelter or shelters that are used. The piecing together of a plan that is acceptable to the patient and that is possible with limited resources is a challenge.

Zacharias[14] at the Hermann Hospital, a 750-bed teaching institution in Houston, Texas, writes of a weekly "nonresource" meeting. The meeting was initially between the patient financial services department and the social work department, but because of an increase in patient acuity levels and in uncompensated care, it has now expanded to include the nursing service department. Zacharias tells of formal aftercare arrangements such as with

- a rehabilitation hospital that, for every paying patient referred from Hermann Hospital, gives dollar credits that can be used for indigent patients from that hospital; and
- a local hotel near the hospital that provides special daily rates for kidney transplant patients who do not live in the immediate area. Reimbursement for the kidney transplant workup is limited, and therefore the workup is most cost-effectively done on an outpatient basis.[15]

Informal arrangements such as the hospital providing medications until the patient is approved for Medicaid, or loaning a wheelchair to a rehabilitation patient, or paying for rental of an apnea monitor are examples of the hospital's assisting on a temporary basis with the meeting of continuing care needs. Developing these possible solutions to care needs requires the continuing care professional to be open, flexible, creative, and a boundary-spanner both within the hospital system and between the hospital and the community.

Discharge planning from acute care involves more than just referrals to community agencies. It involves the development of coalitions among facilities and agencies and among all health care providers. The emphasis must be on meeting care needs and developing and strengthening resources.

NOTES

1. Bernice C. Harper, "Continuity of Care," *Hospitals* April 1, 1973, pp. 115–18.

2. Frank Baker and Herbert C. Schulberg, "Community Health Care-Giving Systems: Integration of Interorganizational Networks," in *Systems and Medical Care,* ed. Alan Sheldon, Frank Baker, and Curtis P. McLaughlin (Cambridge, Mass.: MIT Press, 1970), p. 195.

3. Angela R. Falcone, *Long-Term Care Information System Assessment Process* (Lansing, Mich.: Michigan Office of Services to the Aging, 1978), p. 1. Funded by W. K. Kellogg Foundation, Grant #5000.

4. Ibid., p. 69.

5. Ibid.

6. Conference Report to Accompany H.R. 5300, OBRA of 1986. (October 17, 1986), Section 9305, p. 125.

7. Ibid.

8. Ibid.

9. *Discharge Planning Manual,* 2d ed. (Morristown, N.J.: Morristown Memorial Hospital, 1984), p. 7.

10. Patricia A. O'Hare, "Examining the Discharge Planning Process: An Evaluation of Two Models in an Acute Care Community Hospital" (Ph.D. diss., The Johns Hopkins University School of Hygiene and Public Health, 1984).

11. Ruth E. Lindenberg and Claudia Coulton, "Planning for Posthospital Care: A Follow-up Study," *Health and Social Work* 5, no. 1 (February 1980), pp. 45–50.

12. David R. Dintenfass and Ronald Winter, "Preventive Discharge Planning," *Discharge Planning Update,* November-December 1986, pp. 19–23.

13. Ibid., pp. 20–21.

14. Lee Zacharias, "Indigent Care: An Aggressive Approach," *Discharge Planning Update,* May–June 1987, p. 1.

15. Ibid., pp. 7–8.

Chapter 8

Discharge Planning in the Nursing Home

Lester W. Scheuermann

8

The nursing home's response to effective discharge planning has been, at best, fragmented and, more often, nonexistent. A major contributing factor to this response is a widely accepted belief that nursing homes are the last homes for the aged. This view is a carry-over from a time when nursing homes were used in the absence of all societal supports: families traditionally assumed the responsibility of taking care of a chronically ill relative. Nursing homes were viewed as a necessary evil. The sociological shift from the extended to the nuclear family and the advent of direct government funding (Medicare and Medicaid programs) for nursing home care have established the nursing home as a more convenient, if not acceptable, form of long-term care.

Long-term care can have two purposes: rehabilitation and custodial. A nursing home stay for rehabilitation purposes is acceptable in society, and the costs are often covered by Medicare and some commercial policies. These nursing homes are often referred to as "rehabilitation facilities." Long-term care for rehabilitation is usually limited to people with disabilities that have a good prognosis for improvement, such as a fractured hip or newly diagnosed stroke. Nursing home stays that are likely to last longer than three months, however, are almost never covered by these health insurances and tend to be viewed as permanent. The only insurance coverage for these long-staying residents is Medicaid, an entitlement program generally referred to as "welfare," which pays for some or all of the nursing home costs for about two-thirds of residents.[1]

Nursing homes are an example of total institutions that tend to minimize independence and individuality and foster a high level of dependency on the institution itself.[2] Those who enter nursing homes are dependent already and are often confronted with the most significant loss experienced by a person: the loss of decision-making control over their lives, a loss of responsibility for themselves.[3] The institutional life style, however humane, is often overwhelming for many people who are unable to cope with the high degree of required conformity. Feeling helpless and faced with what they perceive as a hopeless situation, they may become more debilitated and even die within several months of entering the facility.[4]

Government regulations and funding have served to raise the standards for care in most homes and were instrumental in the construction of many new nursing homes.[5] Although government intervention is essential to ensure a minimum standard of care, it has been a rather myopic approach to long-term care. The nursing home has become the only fully funded program for national long-term care. In addition, to ensure that funding was used appropriately, agencies were created to certify that only people who needed an intermediate or skilled level of care[6] would qualify. The presumption, at least on a federal level, is that a person either is very dependent, thus requiring nursing home care, or is independent and could live alone in the community. It is not uncommon for the hospital discharge planning staff to have to look carefully when assessing a person to ensure that that person, who is a borderline case and cannot safely return to the community, receives an intermediate level of care. The determination of levels of care continues after the person is placed in the nursing home. Even reluctant nursing homes have been forced to face the reality of discharge planning.

The success of any discharge planning program lies in the knowledge, skill, and commitment of its staff as well as in the strong support of the agency's administration. Discharge planning in nursing homes is primarily the responsibility of the social work staff, who do not necessarily perceive this as a high priority. In homes that have full-time social workers, they are usually too few to adequately resolve individual and family psychosocial problems in addition to taking on the responsibility of assessing and planning for discharge from the institution. They may also be expected to function as an adjunct to nursing staff to bring about appropriate individual or family behavior changes for the efficient operation of the institution. If discharge planning is attempted, the staff may lack the knowledge and skill to use state-of-the-art approaches for effective implementation. The nursing home's identity as a "home" for its "residents" tends to reinforce the permanency with which the institution and its staff perceive the person's stay. It is only by exception that people leave, and often only when the home is faced with a potential denial of payment owing to improvements in the person's level of care.

Another factor that hampers discharge planning is the lack of community support. Often the family members are present and supportive but only to the extent that the institution assumes primary responsibility for day-to-day care. Family members are usually unwilling or unable to provide the kind of supervision and care needed by many people in a nursing home.[7]

When a family is motivated, there is often a lack of reimbursed, adequate, long-term care community resources. An example of this would be the person who cannot qualify for a skilled nursing need for Medicare reimbursement for a home health agency's intervention. In some states Medicaid may provide limited assistance, but only if the person is financially eligible.[8]

Often family members may have sustained a person in the community before the nursing home placement. They may have anguished over the decision but usually accept it as the only alternative, and even feel relief afterward. The thought of having to resume what they perceive as a major stress is frightening. Often families, acting with the best of intentions, have disposed of the person's home and furnishings. Families are usually advised to do so by social workers in order to ensure continued Medicaid eligibility for the nursing home care. This has presented added stress for the nursing home in attempting to return a person to the community and may also further enhance the sense of hopelessness in the person.

Perhaps the most widely used community resources for nursing home discharge planning are the community residential facilities (CRFs), or foster homes. These facilities provide a supervised environment but no nursing services. Individual residents are expected to perform their activities of daily living and administer their own medication. Some states offer partial, although usually minimal, supplemental funding. Many offer nothing and do not regulate such homes, leaving open the possibility of abuse and exploitation. In the absence of this regulation, nursing homes may be even more reluctant to initiate discharge planning to such facilities, since it may be difficult to evaluate and ensure the quality of care provided. There are currently no other types of facility that provide inpatient services at any level below the intermediate nursing home level of care. In addition, when low-rent senior housing may be appropriate, it is generally unavailable.

Studies indicate that between 20 and 40 percent of intermediate care nursing home residents could be adequately cared for in the community if alternative resources were available.[9] For example, assistance with medication management could replace a service currently provided at the intermediate level of nursing home care.

MODEL

Effective discharge planning models must begin with a change in social policy that will increase funding for alternatives to nursing home care. At the core of this change should be the priority of the person's psychosocial needs over financial considerations; this will encourage the development of more extensive community-based long-term care programs. One such program might be a residential facility that would bridge the gap between nursing home and CRF. People who are in need of medication management and assistance with some activities of daily living could be cared for by licensed practical nurses and aides in such a facility. Because the facility could function similarly to a CRF, its overhead costs could be significantly lower. The reimbursement rate would be high enough to encourage private development of such facilities yet significantly below the cost of a nursing home, thus being potentially cost-effective.

Improvements in social policy do not necessarily result in high financial expenditures. As noted earlier, the current system of reimbursement for long-term care and the lack of available community supports, such as affordable housing, implicitly confine many people to nursing homes permanently. An innovative, cost-effective approach might include a financial incentive to nursing homes to encourage aggressive discharge planning; interagency coordination of services that would link senior housing, case management, Medicaid and community social service departments; and aide services that would initially be available on an intensive daily basis. Although the costs of these programs might exceed the per diem nursing home rate, they would be tapered off within six months until the person would be receiving standard community benefits.

The most fundamental change required of nursing home staff is a change in attitude about discharge planning. Discharge planning should be directly linked with functional goals that would be established for every person on entering the facility. This approach would open the possibility for more people to be considered for eventual discharge. It would also represent a reversal of the current approach of considering only those who clearly stand out as not appropriate for continued nursing home care or who are at risk for losing their certification at intermediate level of care. In order to accomplish this the nursing home administration needs to be committed to enhancing the staff's knowledge and skill through appropriate educational programs.

All staff members who care for a person should be involved in the discharge planning process, which requires a multidisciplinary approach. At the very least the nurses in charge as well as the discharge planning staff should be expected to support an aggressive, innovative program whose goal is to return any resident to the community when appropriate supports are identified.

It is possible to develop an effective model within the confines of current social policy that does little to encourage effective discharge planning in nursing homes. As stated earlier, it is imperative that the nursing home administration be committed to discharge planning and that a qualified discharge planner be given the latitude necessary to implement changes and educate the staff.

The discharge planning process should begin in the preadmission phase, during which both the person and his or her family are most receptive to intervention. They may still be discussing the need for placement and the alternatives available. Unresolved family developmental issues may abound that give rise to feelings of guilt and a sense of responsibility. Behavioral changes may occur, ranging from avoidance or denial to blatant manipulation. By effectively engaging the person and his or her family or social supports, the groundwork for increased support in the nursing home is laid as well as the possibility of support for a potential discharge. Failure to engage in this preadmission process increases the possibility that the placement will be essentially indefinite.[10]

After the person is admitted to the nursing home, the social supports should be encouraged and nurtured to remain actively involved with the person's care. Regular family conferences and educational programs will maximize their cooperation with discharge planning. If the discharge plan involves having a person reside with his or her family, the family could be encouraged to begin by gradually having the person in the home for progressively longer overnight visits. This may, however, require a change of the Medicaid policy, which limits the number of overnight visits.

A thorough, ongoing, multidisciplinary assessment of the person's functional status is the basis for any established goals and therapeutic intervention. At this point the discharge planner would be working closely with the nursing and therapy staff for day-to-day care. Certain dysfunctions, such as incontinence and disorientation, yield a poor prognosis for discharge planning, and thus require maximum intervention, which may include bladder and bowel training and reality orientation.[11]

The person's affective state will significantly influence the possibility of discharge. Depression, a common disorder in nursing homes, can influence the person's motivation to achieve established goals. It is therefore important to perform a thorough assessment and respond with appropriate intervention, such as counseling and antidepressant therapy.

The needs and desires of the person need to be the starting point for discharge planning. People who perceive control over their lives will tend to respond by accepting more responsibility and are more willing to take initiative and risks. In appropriately supporting the person's desires, the discharge planner functions as a "client advocate" and may even empower the person to persuasively engage social supports for assistance in resolving difficulties surrounding the discharge plan.

The final hurdle in planning for a discharge is the identification of appropriate environmental supports. Given the current limitation in resources, much will be left to the planner's knowledge and ingenuity. One creative approach might be for the nursing home to enter into a cooperative agreement with one or more CRFs, thus enabling the home to place people with a minimum of difficulty. A similar arrangement with a home health agency could also have the advantage of ensuring an effective continuum of care, assuming that the care needs are reimbursable.

CONCLUSION

Discharge planning in nursing homes has been largely neglected owing to negative attitudes associated with nursing home care and the lack of financial support for alternative forms of long-term care. Changes in social policy will encourage more effective approaches to discharge planning, but the potential exists for nursing homes to establish a model that will encompass all of the essential elements of an effective discharge planning program. This model can return more people to the community and can improve cooperation among the person, the family, and the staff. A secondary benefit to the home lies in the positive public and community relations that can be associated with a facility that has an effective discharge planning model.

The ultimate beneficiary of effective discharge planning will be the person who may be able to derive some hope in what was previously a hopeless situation.

NOTES

1. Institute of Medicine, Committee on Nursing Home Regulation, *Improving the Quality of Care in Nursing Homes* (Washington, D.C.: National Academy Press, 1986), p. 194.
2. Sheldon S. Tobin and Mortin A. Lieberman, *Last Home for the Aged* (San Francisco: Jossey-Bass Publishers, 1978), pp. 10–14.
3. Susan Mercer and Rosalie Kane, "Helplessness and Hopelessness Among the Institutionalized Aged: An Experiment," *Health and Social Work* 1, no. 1 (February 1979): 93.
4. C. Knight Aldrich, "Personality Factors and Mortality in the Relocation of the Aged," *Gerontologist* 4, no. 2 (June 1964): 93.
5. Elias S. Cohen, "An Overview of Long-Term Care Facilities," in *A Social Work Guide for Long-term Care Facilities*, ed. Elaine M. Brody (Rockville, Md.: U.S. Department of Health, Education, and Welfare, 1974), pp. 12–21.

6. *Skilled:* Requiring continuous skilled nursing care or rehabilitation therapy provided by a registered nurse or therapist in a residential facility. *Intermediate:* Requiring continuous health-related services in a residential facility with minimal or no services provided by a registered nurse or therapist.

7. Brody, *A Social Work Guide,* p. 119.

8. U.S. General Accounting Office, Office of Comptroller General, *Entering a Nursing Home—Costly Implications for Medicaid and the Elderly* (Washington, D.C.: November 1979), p. 30.

9. U.S. General Accounting Office, *The Elderly Should Benefit from Expanded Home Health Care but Increasing These Services Will Not Insure Cost Reductions* (Washington, D.C.: December 1982), p. 9.

10. Lucille Alan, "The Importance of Including the Family in the Comprehensive Psychiatric Assessment of the Nursing Home Bound Person," *Journal of Gerontological Social Work* 7, no. 3 (May 1984): 37.

11. Mary Ann Lewis, Robert L. Kane, Shan Cretin, et al., "The Immediate and Subsequent Outcomes of Nursing Home Care," *American Journal of Public Health* 75, no. 7 (July 1985): 759.

Chapter 9

Discharge Planning from the Home Health Agency

Susan Coleman

9

Discharge planning is no longer limited to use in hospitals and nursing homes. Now a formalized discharge planning program is also essential for home health agencies. In examining discharge planning from a home health agency perspective, and in understanding the reasons for its increasing importance, an operational definition of home health care is necessary. For the purposes of this discussion, home health care is skilled, intermittent care provided to essentially homebound people as defined under the Medicare guidelines.

The Medicare model, whose standards have been adopted by many private and commercial insurance carriers, is based on the requirement for short-term restorative treatment. Many Blue Cross and Blue Shield policies carry this interpretation a step further by stipulating that home care will be covered only in lieu of hospitalization. Therefore, the following section involving discharge planning from the home health agency applies not only to Medicare beneficiaries, but also to most other carriers with a home health benefit.

Discharge planning from home health care agencies, as a formalized practice, is one of the more recent concepts in the industry. Its further development, however, is imperative for financial, legal, and quality assurance reasons.

Home health care agencies certified under the Medicare program are required to have written policies relating both to the acceptance of patients into home care and to consideration for discharging, or terminating services to their patients. These policies must cover such issues as patient notification of service termination, documentation of the reason for discharge, and physician notification and concurrence with the plan for termination. Generally a statement is included in the policy regarding the necessity for a discharge to occur after arrangements for continuing care or follow-up services have been completed.

Although such policies currently exist in the home care industry, the processes undertaken are often less than formal. Many agencies lack the basic mechanisms needed to complete discharge planning. An additional factor contributing to these inadequacies in the process is the basic lack of community resources available to support patients once they become ineligible for home care. Owing in part to the lack of systems and in part to the lack of resources, patients are often maintained on home care service rolls after their eligibility lapses.

Medicare patients receiving skilled care who develop longer-term maintenance requirements usually have to gain Medicaid eligibility or privately pay for continuing care, including the possibility of nursing home care.[1] Surprisingly, however, only 2 percent of home care patients are discharged to nursing home care. The most vital resource currently available to those planning discharges from home health agencies is the patient's family. Two-thirds of home care patients live with family members, and are discharged to a level of care that involves relatives as their support systems.

A thorough examination of the need for and the trend toward formalizing mechanisms for discharge planning from home health care is not complete without a study of the incentives to create and develop such processes. The reasons for an increased need in this area fall into several categories: financial, legal, Medicare compliance, marketing, and quality assurance.

FINANCIAL

Reimbursement to home health agencies for the provision of skilled services has decreased. Even before the Gramm-Rudman federal budget cuts, home health care had felt the financial squeeze. Medicare, the payer in nearly 80 percent of the patient caseload in most agencies, reimburses home health care on a cost-based system. The Gramm-Rudman cuts decrease reimbursement by a percentage across the board to a level that is essentially below cost.

This system of reimbursement to providers is clearly an incentive to begin planning for a patient's discharge right from admission. To keep a patient under home health services beyond the point of coverage is detrimental to the agency's fiscal well-being.

Many skilled home health agencies are also equipped with a private duty, or private pay, sector. Frequently these entities are formed as separate corporations in order to be profit-producing rather than cost-based companies. An additional financial incentive for a strong discharge planning program in the skilled agency involves shifting patients to the private pay sector whenever feasible. By maximizing, but not overextending, the patients' skilled home health benefit and then "discharging" them to the private duty nursing corporation, losses can be avoided and profits maximized.

The Health Care Financing Administration is considering imposing regulations on the home health care industry to decrease costs by encouraging provider efficiency. Just as a similar move resulted in a prospective payment system for hospitals in 1982, it is likely that prospective payment will also be imposed on home health care in the near future.

After the onset of prospective payment in hospitals a struggle ensued to develop programs and systems to effectively deal with the effects of this legislation. Discharge planning was one of the most significant and important of the developing systems. Home health agencies will be similarly affected if and when a prospective payment system is instituted. Strong discharge planning programs will likewise be key factors to ensure agency survival.

LEGAL

Home health care agencies have a responsibility to their patients to assure appropriate termination of services and proper referral to follow-up care. An agency can be charged with abandonment if certain conditions of discharge are not met.

In order to avoid a charge of abandonment, an agency must give patients reasonable alternatives for care, or a reasonable amount of time to find alternative care, before discharge from the agency. The care alternatives and the warnings for impending discharge must be adequately documented in the patient's record.

The issue of abandonment, and the fact that such suits have been brought against agencies, brings an important legal consideration to the forefront. A well-developed discharge planning program safeguards home health agencies from the likelihood of an avoidable abandonment suit.

Home health agencies, when accepting a patient for care, become the patient's case manager. As such, they are responsible for coordinating care from case acceptance through discharge and appropriate aftercare referrals. With this responsibility comes a legal liability. Charges can also be made against an agency for failure to fulfill this role. Again, proper discharge planning can avert at least a portion of the risk involved as a case manager.

MEDICARE COMPLIANCE

A further issue necessitating discharge planning within the home care agency involves compliance with the Medicare regulations. The Medicare Conditions of Participation mandate a discharge policy and discharge summary. Further, the standardized plan of treatment forms (commonly referred to as the 485, 486, and 487 forms) instituted in 1985 mandate completion of a section called "Discharge Plan."

In order to adequately comply with the regulations, a minimal knowledge of discharge planning is necessary. In order to maximize the usefulness and effectiveness of the plan of treatment, an organized and systematized approach to discharge planning is mandatory.

MARKETING

A strong discharge planning program can give an agency a competitive edge in a free market of home care providers. Proper planning for a discharge generally leaves a patient more prepared for the withdrawal of home health services, and therefore can increase consumer satisfaction. The spread of this satisfaction by word of mouth can be an excellent community relations tool.

Generally speaking, program development assists in giving agencies an advantage in today's competitive atmosphere. Discharge planning is one such program whose development can assist an agency in its marketing strategy.

QUALITY ASSURANCE

Last, but not least, in the list of incentives to develop a home health care discharge planning program is the issue of quality care. Most experts would agree that optimal care requires continuity in any setting. Whether dealing with the transition from hospital to home care, or from home care to custodial support care, the planning and preparation involved in each transfer is equally important in terms of its impact on quality.

The agency's role as case manager has not only legal, but also quality assurance implications. Total case management, including follow-through with discharge planning, is important for the assurance of quality care.

A MODEL FOR DISCHARGE PLANNING

In structuring the mechanisms necessary to conduct an effective discharge planning program from a home health care agency, many of the concepts familiar to hospital systems apply. For example, discharge planning should be initiated early. It is appropriate to begin planning the discharge on admission to the home health agency.

In the home health care model the registered nurse serves as both primary caregiver and case manager. A discharge planning model using the nurse as continuity of care coordinator is most logical. In cases with physical, speech, or occupational therapy involvement, input from these disciplines is also necessary. Additional coordination with the physician, community resources, and, very important, the family is essential. Case conferences may also be indicated with certain patients.

Sometimes the nurse may require assistance with a particularly difficult patient or discharge problem. In such cases social work assistance may be necessary. Under the Medicare home care model, services of a medical social worker are covered for limited intervention in an emotional, a financial, or other problem that interferes with a patient's recuperation. Because social work is not a primary service under Medicare, discharge planning cannot be properly coordinated by that discipline. Using the social worker as a consultant to the nurse is most fitting in the home care model.

Documentation in home health care is of utmost importance. Aside from the reimbursement and legal reasons, it is truly the main indicator that the agency has to evaluate staff performance, use of services, and quality of care rendered. Documentation of discharge planning must be ongoing and consistent. It can be included in the nurse's narrative note, or separated out onto a flow chart. Either way the documentation must include evidence of discharge planning and address the following: progress toward goals, continued needs of the patient, plan for meeting the needs, family and physician involvement, and the time frame allotted to accomplish the discharge plan and goals.

Finally, a model for discharge planning from the home health agency must include a mechanism for quality assurance. In order to assess the discharge planning process, an evaluation component should be added to the required utilization review or quality assurance format. Using questions such as those that follow during chart reviews can assure proper discharge planning by means of a documentation evaluation:

- When did discharge planning begin?
- Did the decision to discharge reflect a logical development of the plan of care, service goals, continuity of care, and physician coordination?

- Did the patient and/or his or her family participate in planning the discharge?
- Did the discharge result in any way from agency or staff limitations?
- Were any other community resources used in the plan for discharge? If yes, specify.

In conclusion, discharge planning in home care, now in its infancy, must soon come of age. As discussed, discharge planning is a matter of necessity, not one of choice for home health agencies. The concepts more familiar to the acute care setting need to be modified for the community and put into everyday use.

NOTES

1. M. Mundinger, *Home Care Controversy: Too Little, Too Late, Too Costly* (Rockville, Md.: Aspen Publishers, 1983), p. 172.

Chapter 10

A New Approach to Continuity of Care from the Physician's Office

Michael P. O'Brien

10

HISTORICAL PERSPECTIVE

In 1978 a group of physicians on the staff of Pacific Presbyterian Medical Center in San Francisco embarked on a project that would have far more effects on the delivery of medical care in their practices than they could have imagined. Instead of combining their financial resources and hiring a project management firm to develop and build a new medical office building, the physicians decided to form a limited partnership, Pan Med Enterprises, to plan and develop their own building. As if this was not in and of itself challenging enough, they took the time and dedication to ensure that this would not be just another medical office building. The physicians set the tone of their endeavor by seeking suggestions from people who were involved with the development, planning, and delivery of innovative health care. One of the provocative ideas put forth at that time was to develop a suite in the building to deal with the nonmedical needs and the social, emotional, and psychological difficulties that patients face when beset by illness or disability. The idea became reality several years later in 1984, when the Patient Assistance Foundation was incorporated as an independent nonprofit group dedicated to the provision of those services, offering counseling, guidance, and support to patients and families. The Foundation Board, consisting of physicians and community leaders, took as its primary mission the establishment of the Office of Patient Services, which would be the direct provider for those nonmedical services.

In 1986 the Pacific Presbyterian Professional Building opened its doors on the original site of the Stanford Medical School. The building is owned and operated by the 150 physicians who occupy it, and covers the full range of medical specialties. In addition to physician suites, it houses a clinical laboratory, a radiology suite, and a professional pharmacy—all of which are owned by the Pacific Presbyterian Medical Center, which is a 341-bed acute care facility noted for its excellence in ophthalmology, transplantation, care of AIDS patients, and the Planetree Model Hospital Project, to name a few. The physicians who were involved in the development of the professional building worked closely with the administration of the hospital during the development of the building to ensure that only the highest standards of medical care would be met in this major undertaking.

THE OFFICE OF PATIENT SERVICES

The Patient Assistance Foundation has sought to develop the Office of Patient Services (OPS) as a model for nonmedical patient service delivery in a private practice setting. With recent shifts toward outpatient, ambulatory disease management, patient services has become critical in providing continuity of care to outpatients and case management services. The services are currently paid for by using funds provided by a grant from the medical center. The exciting focus of OPS can best be described by the following critical elements:

• Provides services as an "extension" of the physician's office
• Utilizes the case management model
• Maintains direct community interaction
• Acts as a liaison with the medical center.

The Foundation manages OPS as an opportunity to provide an exceptional service in an era replete with cutbacks in soft services.

The OPS occupies 1,625 square feet on the lobby level of the professional building and houses space for private offices, a conference room, a patient library, consultation areas, and an audiovisual instruction area. Special attention was taken to use colors and materials that would project a warm and pleasant atmosphere to the patients and visitors who use the facility.

The staff of the office includes a nurse, a social worker, a part-time nutritionist, two receptionists, an office manager, and the executive director.

Since OPS was to represent the "caring" focus of the professional building, the Board of Directors of Pan Med asked it to administrate the delivery of reception services in the main lobby. Information, directions, and wheelchair loan are offered by the two receptionists to all visitors. Such services are actively provided to the large number of elderly or disabled patients who visit daily. This "enabling" resource allows patients to be welcomed to the campus as well as to establish a route that would best suit their needs. Located close to the entrance of the building, these receptionists also provide physician referrals and triage to OPS when the need is apparent.

In the area of health education, the OPS nurse offers patients and groups a gradual introduction to understanding their disease and treatment. Instruction may be given for such conditions as renal failure, inflammatory bowel disorders, and eye diseases. Under physician direction the nurse provides patients with a broader understanding of surgical preparation and information on diagnostic procedures. For example, a patient who is to undergo sigmoidoscopy or a similar procedure meets with the nurse educator to view a videotape about the test. The nurse then answers questions and discusses what the results may mean to the person. This nurse also offers drug information and counseling, general guidance regarding specific disease-related diets, pulmonary rehabilitation counseling, and health promotion opportunities to those who want to change their life styles.

The counseling component of OPS is carried out by the social worker. Using the case management model, the social worker avoids duplication of service by linking patients with existing community resources. Except for instances of crisis intervention, the worker provides no ongoing psychotherapy. As their case manager, the social worker prepares depressed patients for therapy by helping them focus on issues that have caused their sense of helplessness, inquiring about their insurance coverage for mental health benefits, and generally abbreviates the "intake" process, which can be so difficult for patients to negotiate. The social worker also offers a wide range of other services, including long-term planning for placement or home care, financial and insurance counseling and referral, legal information and referral, assistance with transportation and overnight lodging accommodations, interpreter services, and adult protective and child protective referrals.

The nutritionist consultations at OPS are provided on a case-by-case basis by a registered dietitian on the staff of the medical center. Patients who have used this service include high-risk cardiac patients, Type I diabetics, pregnant women with weight problems, patients whose weight loss is related to pathology, patients with Crohn's disease, and people who want to improve their general nutrition habits. This service has been welcomed by the physician community in the building where there is precious little time to provide dietary consultation during an office visit.

The OPS has been actively involved with patients since March 24, 1986, and has increased its monthly census by 20 percent per month. Meetings with physicians' office managers and the doctors have yielded for OPS solid recognition of patients' needs as well as suggestions for the addition of other related services, such as chronic illness and bereavement support groups, physician educational coordination, and a formal diabetic teaching program.

In order to offer a more comprehensive model for continuity of care on the Pacific Presbyterian Medical Center (PPMC) campus, a significant amount of time has been invested in the development of relationships between OPS and hospital departments. This process has included input to and from social services, nursing, administration, Board of Trustees, division of education, the patient education committee, admissions, transport, dietary, and others with whom OPS has frequent contact. The cultivation of these relationships has been extremely important for both sides, since patients and families must be offered comprehensive care no matter how many departments or agencies on the same campus they visit. This has often been the problem with turf-dominated systems, in which patients "belong" to one or another service. Such is not the case on the PPMC campus. The OPS and the medical center have made a conscious effort to interact positively in order to project to patients that the system exists for their benefit, not to challenge them.

IMPACT ON CONTINUITY OF CARE

The OPS was developed as a specific linkage for the physician's office, the hospital, and the community. During its developmental phase, people representing all three areas were asked to meet with planners to contribute ideas and support to this dynamic new opportunity to lend guidance to patients and families. This methodology put aside many turf-related concerns and allowed participants to mold this new service that would counsel, inform, educate, and generally respond to a more skeptical health care consumer.

For some time the Medical Center's Department of Social Services was frequently asked by physicians to consult on ambulatory patients who had difficulty with transportation to a physician's office or who needed extensive social service management because of long-term care needs. Not having the staff resources to cope with such requests, the department clearly outlined a significant role for OPS.

Once OPS became a reality, the role it would play became even more distinct. The continuity of care system between the physician's office and the hospital, and vice versa, had been a difficult one in which to provide direct follow-up. Because of the never-ending cycle of admissions and discharges, hospital discharge planners would be taxed just to develop a plan for a high-risk patient. There was often minimal follow-up time available to evaluate how the patient fared at home. Similarly, the physician's office found it difficult to monitor how the patient and family were coping relative to the proposed discharge plan. The OPS has provided that vital link that prepares the patient and family for admission into the hospital and then transfers the case to the discharge planning team for their professional management. Similarly, on discharge, the case is transferred back to the OPS team of professionals, who interact with the patient, caretakers, home care providers, and physician's office to ensure that the delicate balance of care is present to prevent readmission or transfer to a long-term care facility.

From this description one can see that there are many advantages to utilization of a system similar to OPS. They include the following:

- Enriched preparation for location of care
- More visible on-campus linkage with physician's office and hospital
- Identifiable contact for community agencies to link to physician community
- Defined involvement of patient and support system
- Strengthening of the patient's role as a consumer of health care
- Enhancement of the physician's and hospital's opportunity to provide "comprehensive" health care

As providers of continuity of care services, many professionals have been consumers caught up in the fragmentation of the delivery system. The OPS model offers a means of continuity that is fairly unavailable in typical situations.

Because examples are often the most effective means of teaching, the following three cases demonstrate continuity of care under this system.

Mrs. W., a 76-year-old widow who lives alone, is referred to the OPS social worker by her physician before admission for gallbladder surgery. She is seeking information on home care arrangements. Although the patient's son would be available before and immediately after surgery, he would not be able to stay to provide ongoing care, since he lives out of the country. The patient was most interested in developing a home health program that she could depend on after discharge. The OPS social worker discussed the various home health services available and explained how the hospital discharge planning system operates. Mrs. W. and her son agreed that a live-in home health aide would be the most appropriate source of assistance to fill her needs. The patient also requested the opportunity to interview various home health agencies, since it seemed uncertain that insurance would cover part or all of the cost of this care. When the patient had finally made an agency selection, this was communicated to the hospital discharge planner, who monitored the patient's case after surgery and made the final arrangements for the initiation of the home care plan. The patient was then transferred back to the OPS social worker, who worked with the patient to gradually reduce aide hours and establish a financial agreement with the agency. The physician's office was constantly aware of this plan as it progressed.

Mr. S., a 64-year-old married Filipino, lives in San Francisco and is retired from the Merchant Marines. He was referred to the OPS nurse by his cardiologist for education regarding a scheduled cardiac catheterization for post–myocardial infarction studies. The nurse gave Mr. S. the opportunity to verbalize his fears regarding the test and what the findings may mean. Only then, after the patient had expressed his anxiety, did the nurse explain to him educational material that described his upcoming procedure. The OPS nurse then contacted the short stay surgery unit at the medical center to make arrangements for the staff to be prepared for the patient and to reinforce the continuity of outpatient education. If necessary, this educational process can be carried into the hospital admission. Mr. S. was calm during the procedure and aftercare, attributing much of this to the preparation and insight he received from the nurse.

Mrs. H., a 63-year-old widow, was referred to the OPS nurse by her orthopedic surgeon to secure information on total hip replacement. The patient had had a bilateral mastectomy three months before, after which she began a walking program. Mrs. H. subsequently developed left hip pain, and x-ray revealed damage, making hip replacement necessary. The nurse viewed two videos with the patient, describing the procedure and aftercare, which she found quite helpful. The patient was also instructed on the discharge planning program at the medical center and was asked to consider what her needs might be before surgery. The OPS nurse also alerted the hospital discharge planners to the patient's possible need for assistance near discharge and visited the patient during her hospitalization. The hospital staff nurses noted how well the patient had done and credited the educational preparation she had before surgery. The patient was discharged home with an uncomplicated home health plan, and a follow-up phone call from the OPS nurse found her to be recovering with minimal anxiety and discomfort.

Mrs. B., a 44-year-old divorcée, was referred to OPS by her physician before her discharge from the hospital. The patient was hospitalized for

Crohn's disease and injuries related to alcohol-related seizures. Her physician asked the OPS social worker to become involved with the patient before discharge. The patient was experiencing a number of problems, including housing, disability, divorce-related depression, lack of health insurance, unemployment, and alcohol abuse. The social worker met with the patient and contacted the discharge planners, and together they worked out arrangements for a safe home care plan. After discharge the patient and the social worker remained in contact by way of telephone and office visits and gradually began to solve the patient's many problems. All efforts to correct these issues were reinforced by the physician's office and seemed to strengthen the patient's impression that her physician was interested in her "total" care.

As these examples indicate, the continuity of care available through OPS is unique. In a cost-effective, multidisciplinary, single-office setting these services are provided to patients, demonstrating a difficult-to-deliver dedication to comprehensive care. Also made clear in these cases is the importance of the preadmission work done by the clinical staff. In recent years continuity-of-care providers have given admissions preparation more attention but found it difficult to accomplish with the "quicker and sicker" discharge planning stress. The OPS experience thus far strengthens the notion that in order to provide more efficient and comprehensive discharge planning, health care professionals must lend as much attention to admissions. The location of this responsibility in an agency that represents the physician's office is most appropriate, since admission and discharge timing often depends on the physician's authority and professional judgment.

SUMMARY

Discharge planning from the physician's office setting has been difficult to structure and maintain in the traditional sense of the process. However, with an emerging population of Americans who are more educated about their health care and expect more from it, the physician is being looked to more frequently for answers that he or she may not have. The physician community who came together to research and direct the establishment of the OPS saw some distinct benefits associated with this type of delivery of health care. These include the following:

- Increased access by patients to services they see as necessary to their informed consumer role

Exhibit 10-1 Impact on Continuity of Care

- Stronger mandate from consumer and physician
- Less breakdown resulting in placement or rehospitalization
- Enriched preparation for location of care
- Encourages involvement of patient and support system
- More visible linkage with hospital
- Identifiable contact for community agencies
- Liaison to and from physician
- Enhanced physician and hospital accountability
- Provides distance for evaluations
- Strengthens patient's power base

- Increased coordination of patient care both to and from the hospital or home
- Improved continuity to an otherwise fragmented delivery system (see Exhibit 10-1)
- Placed some responsibility back into the hands of the patient by providing the tools, resources, and education to effectively manage his or her own care
- Provided a specific response to the meaning of "total" care by incorporating the educational and social services within the medical system
- Provided services that normally were available only to hospital inpatients
- Provided convenient on-site opportunity to use these services recommended by their physician

---

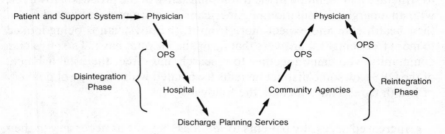

Figure 10-1 OPS Continuity of Care Model

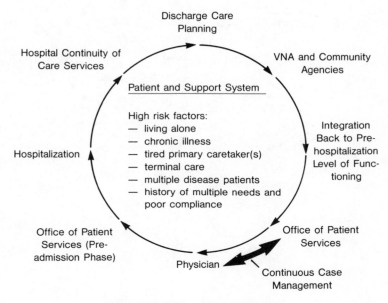

Figure 10-2 Office of Patient Services

- Improved the quality of care by upgrading the education about illness and treatment
- Made an abundance of resources accessible to patients of all social, cultural, and economic sectors regardless of their ability to pay

Finally, this innovative model (see Figure 10-1) is one that our health care system has attempted to incorporate, sometimes unsuccessfully because of various other pressures, such as communication and coordination. Although physicians have been taught that their primary role is to educate, and they strive to do so, it is often impossible to provide significant depth for every patient. The OPS makes this more realistic by extending the practice of the physician into a new, exciting area that does provide continuity of care in a consumer-enriched environment (see Figure 10-2).

Chapter 11

Discharge Planning Models and Strategies in an HMO

Kay L. Rogers

11

Health Maintenance Organizations (HMOs), Preferred Provider Organizations (PPOs), and Exclusive Provider Organizations (EPOs) are examples of today's managed health care system. The goal of these organnizations is to unify the control of quality and cost of care. Specifically, an HMO provides or arranges for the provision of health services to its enrollees through designated providers for a prepaid capitated fee.

An HMO is a *system* of care that unifies the traditionally fragmented settings (e.g., inpatient, physician's office, nursing home, and home sites) in order to provide continuity and quality of care in a cost-effective mode. As provider and insurer of the member's care, the HMO also has an incentive to translate quality and efficiently managed care into terms that are meaningful to employer groups and individual members. Discharge planning's role in an HMO is to develop strategies to meet both challenges: to provide quality, appropriate, cost-effective care and to maintain a competitive product in the marketplace. Quality, appropriateness, and cost-effectiveness are attributes that must be reflected in the services established for the member. Discharge planners gather and synthesize information regarding the members' hospitalization, current and projected health status, and levels of available medical, nursing, or rehabilitative support. Moving members to a safe and competent level of health care is then facilitated. Quality care is the primary factor in influencing the discharge planning team's decisions. Without quality being factored into the continuum of care, appropriate and cost-effective services would be impossible to attain.

To operationalize appropriate care, discharge planners facilitate the transfer of members to settings that can meet their health care needs with compatible resources. Discharge planners assist in assessing and creatively planning for additional ways to meet a member's care per episode of illness. One of these creative methods involves a transitional care setting located within the hospital. This setting is used between acute hospitalization and home care or nursing home placement. A patient qualifies for transitional care if he or she is medically stable and requires fewer hours of nursing care than most medical-surgical patients. Discharge planners in an HMO can use these integrated levels of care for specific diagnostic categories or individual need. This is a unique advantage to the discharge planner in the HMO setting, since the insurer and caregiver are one and the same and approvals for arranging service are easier to obtain.

Finally, the discharge planner complements the HMO's cost-effectiveness by initiating individualized care plans early in a member's hospitalization. Planning that occurs close to an admission allows the physician, the member, and the health care system an opportunity to prepare for the phases of care. Preparation is vital to avoid omission of needed services. Throughout this planning process the discharge planner considers the relative cost-effectiveness of one plan compared with an alternative. This responsibility requires the discharge planner to have an information baseline regarding rates per setting and service.

Discharge planning is in a unique position in an HMO's health care delivery system. By consistently using these basic parameters of quality appropriateness and cost-effectiveness, the discharge planners can enhance the HMO's viability in the marketplace.

This is the second challenge: to yield a competitive product in the minds of employers and individual consumers. Acknowledging that an HMO's costliest health care product is hospitalization, professional activities that influence the frequency of hospitalizations and length of hospital stays are greatly valued. Discharge planners affect the frequency of hospitalizations in two ways. In some systems the discharge planners function as preadmission assessors. If alternatives to hospitalization are available, one admission may be appropriately avoided. Second, as a comprehensive discharge plan is implemented and meets the patient's outcome goals, a repeat hospitalization is less likely for that episode of illness. Similarly, the lengths of stay in the inpatient setting are largely affected by an HMO's use of discharge planning. By focusing on diminishing the number of nonactivity-producing days (days that medical intervention is not provided) within the hospital, the discharge planners ultimately lower the HMO's expenditures for hospital-based care. Meanwhile the discharge planner also assesses the non–hospital-based care for quality, appropriateness, and cost-effectiveness.

Numerous discharge planning models have been created to confront these challenges. The functional models appear to be in a utilization review base, a quality assurance or service-oriented base, or a hybrid of both.

The utilization review focuses on the number of days or types of service members are using per episode of illness. Discharge planning may be initiated as predetermined length of stay parameters are exceeded. Although emphasis is placed on inpatient facility utilization, outpatient and ancillary service utilization may also be a function of discharge planners' documentation of utilization per member. This contrasts with the quality assurance model, which focuses on the person's assessed needs and facilitates the member's movement through the system. A hybrid discharge planning model involves tailoring of care plans that concurrently impact the length of stay guidelines established by the HMO.

Each of these functional models of discharge planning can be implemented by various personnel. Some HMOs contract with hospital utilization review, quality assurance, or social service departments for discharge planning. The advantage of this choice is to avoid the administrative overhead costs associated with starting a discharge planning department. Other HMOs employ their own discharge planners, who complement the inpatient discharge planning resources. Using HMO personnel provides more system- and insurance-specific information to the discharge plan. These personnel range in backgrounds from nursing, to social service, to more clerical-based personnel (depending on the degree of integration with contracted services). The model of the discharge planning program varies with the type and mission of the HMO. An example of discharge planning in a predominantly staff model HMO (in which the HMO employs the physicians) follows.

Group Health, Inc. (GHI), a consumer-owned and -operated nonprofit HMO, began in 1957. Its 212,000 membership is served by 550 staff and contract physicians at 23 staff and affiliated clinics. A variety of inpatient facilities are used in the Minneapolis metropolitan region; however, patients are primarily concentrated at six facilities. In 1982 GHI identified the need for enhanced coordination and continuity of care for members between the hospital, ambulatory, and home settings.

The GHI home care department committed their public health nurses to work on this objective. This decision was advantageous for GHI because of the public health nurses' knowledge of the HMO and community resources, competency in establishing quality and feasible care plans for posthospitalization, and working relationships and respect with the system's medical staff. The program has grown to five discharge planners with individualized expertise in adult, geriatric, and maternal-child health areas. They are primarily service-oriented discharge planners with some utilization review responsibilities. Therefore, they organizationally are related to both the quality assurance and the utilization review departments. The inpatient professional resources (e.g., social workers, quality assurance staff) work with the HMO's discharge planners in varying degrees.

Given the relatively closed system of care in a staff model, the strengths of this internal discharge planning program are optimized. First, the discharge planner has information regarding each member's care and resources used through access to data, documentation, and consumer feedback. This information serves as an assessment base to develop effective plans. Second, from the physician's management perspective, the physicians have an incentive to use the system's resources (such as the discharge planners' consultations). The physician department leaders support and motivate physicians to work with the discharge planning concepts. The discharge planners and the physicians also use the department leaders to problem-solve complex cases. Third, the discharge planners have access to key components for implementing a discharge plan. A prime asset is the patient. The discharge planners can initiate the assessment process for discharge planning without a physician's order. The following components of most discharge plans are also accessible and used with the physician's authorization: transportation, home care, supplies, and clinic services.

In more open systems, however, discharge planners have to respond to an additional challenge. An open system of managed care is exemplified by an HMO that contracts either with a network or group of physicians or individual physicians. Discharge planning has the same challenge of enhancing quality, appropriate, and cost-effective care while maintaining a marketing edge. The third challenge is to ensure that one's specific HMO's standards of care are met.

There is a potential loss of quality, appropriateness, and cost control owing to the complexity of the open system relationship. The physician associated with the HMO may be participating in more than one managed health plan and may have varied financial relationships per health plan. For example, some participating physicians are financially responsible for all health care costs. Other physicians may be responsible solely for outpatient costs. The HMO must be cognizant of the physician's incentive to participate in managed care. The HMO's discharge planner and the participating physician(s) have to establish priorities for discharge planning interventions. To implement a discharge planning program for these members and physicians, the HMO's discharge planners may be directly involved or serve as consultants to the physician's office personnel. Logistics such as identifying communication pathways and accessing patient data files (e.g., census information) are primary steps to conquer in any discharge planning program. Foremost in the discharge planning process is, however, a commitment by the contracted physician(s) to participate in quality and cost management activities.

In conclusion, HMOs and other managed health care systems greatly depend on discharge planning programs to guide the members and the providers through the system. Continuity and integration of varied levels of care can best be achieved by those outside the direct patient care activity. With the expected growth of managed health care systems, discharge planning is en route to an exciting maturation process!

Chapter 12

Discharge Planning in the Workplace

Margaret A. Terry

12

Private businesses and corporations are now active participants in the health care system. As informed purchasers of health care services, the private sector is either directly or indirectly negotiating for services with providers to obtain quality care at the lowest costs. Businesses are also assisting employees in arranging services for their elderly dependents. These companies are recognizing the complexity and fragmentation of long-term care services as well as the personal and financial burden that elderly care imposes on employees.

Several corporations have taken innovative steps as the prudent purchasers of services. Ciba-Geigy will at times pay physicians more for procedures done outside a hospital. Lockheed is among the companies that require new employees to sign up with health maintenance organizations. Others, such as Quaker Oats, are "dangling carrots" before workers who keep their health care bills to a minimum.[1]

These corporations are offering incentives to physician providers who are in the position of deciding which procedures will be done and designating what provider will do the service. Consumers are also being channeled into choosing less costly insurances and services.

Instead of managing these cost-saving programs, some corporations have hired medical review organizations to handle the administrative aspects. These include preadmission certification for hospital admission and second opinion surgical programs.

One of the most significant of the new approaches is case management. Employees with serious illnesses are offered the help of a consultant to explore the possibility of services being provided in a less expensive manner. This consultant, by discussing options with family and physician, arranges the best care at the least cost. The consultant will often be a nurse, but U.S. Corporate Health Management, a health plan administrator, uses physicians.[2] These employees, retirees, and dependents representing 5 percent of any corporation consume 50 percent of the company's health care dollars.[3]

The incentive for corporations to get into arranging coordinated health plans is the same as for hospitals—cost savings.

Case management programs are mostly voluntary. Corporations and review organizations are new to the business of arranging and coordinating services. Case management offers a cautious and prudent approach as each health plan is tailored to the employee's needs.

Hospital discharge planning programs are usually more aggressive in their approach. Patients are given options and must choose. It would not be surprising to see corporations moving to a penalty system for patients who do not cooperate with the consultant's suggestions. Companies are already doing this in their second opinion surgery programs.

Chrysler, in its innovative approach to skyrocketing health care costs, instituted the following aggressive measures:

- Additional benefits such as vision care will be included only if the employee chooses one of the company's preferred providers.
- Outpatient laboratory benefits will be covered only when tests are done at a specific laboratory. Physicians must order the test at the designated laboratory or the patient pays.
- All employees (including union members) are subject to hospital precertification programs.

The incentives, such as Chrysler's, are changing for all. Physicians will not be paid for services to be delivered where more is better, but will be paid only if services are deemed appropriate. Hospitals now have incentives to discharge sooner for a positive bottom line. Consumers will be directed to where, how much, and by whom to receive their services.

Many of the innovative measures are long overdue, and the purchasers of health care are becoming more knowledgeable about what they can get for their dollar.

The difficulty of arranging long-term chronic care affects both hospital and corporations. Frequently no long-term quality care services are available at a reasonable cost. So corporations need to move cautiously in their new case management programs.

Corporations' participation in the health care system through an "Eldercare" benefit program can benefit them in two ways. They face little risk and financial investment and simultaneously achieve improved relations with employees.

The Corporate Eldercare Project, Older American Initiative, and Elder Services are three programs that provide continuity of care planning and services in the workplace. This movement is still in its infancy but may become the employee benefit of the 1990s.

One of the leaders in the corporate world is the Travelers Company of Hartford, Connecticut. It began its program after surveying 739 home office employees. The survey, considered the first comprehensive study of elderly care at a corporation, found the following:

- One in five employees over age 30 was providing some care to an elderly parent.
- The majority of the employees providing care were women, even when it was the husband's parent.
- The employees on average were providing care for five and a half years and spent ten hours a week fulfilling these responsibilities.
- Eight percent spent 35 or more hours each week.
- Thirty percent provided financial assistance.
- Forty percent managed their parents' finances.
- Four out of five surveyed wanted more information about relevant community resources.[4,5]

The Travelers Company has decided to help employees by offering the following services:

- providing information at a caregiving fair
- providing information and books on caregiving at a corporate library for employees
- lunchtime support groups
- flexible hours
- special video programs on topics such as when to consider a nursing home
- facilitating deductions up to $6,000 a year before taxes to use in caring for an elderly dependent.[6]

The response of the workplace is due to a growing awareness of the stress and financial burden of caring for an elderly relative. This often results in problems at the workplace, such as absenteeism, lateness, and the use of unscheduled days off. Excessive phone use was reported by nearly two-thirds of the employees of companies surveyed by the New

York Business Group on Health.[7] This has most recently become a corporate issue for the following reasons:

- More women now are in the work force and not available for providing care.
- America is aging.
- The long-term system of health and social care for the elderly in the United States is failing.
- Employees frequently don't live close to the elderly relative, and arranging services is even more complicated from a distance.

The major issues faced by the worker are as follows:

- the emotional stress of caregiving for an elderly relative
- the financial burden of paying for nonreimbursed services
- the physical and emotional drain of providing the day-to-day services, transportation, housekeeping, bathing, shopping, cooking, and paperwork
- trying to arrange for quality services in a fragmented, complicated long-term care system.

Other projects exploring the cost and benefits of corporate projects are following Travelers' lead. The University of Bridgeport's Center for the Study of Aging has funding from the Administration on Aging to administer the Corporate Elder Project to four firms: Remington, Pitney Bowes, People's Bank of Bridgeport, and Pepperidge Farm.[8,9] Employees are first surveyed to determine the extent of their responsibilities and the effects on productivity. The project will test several support programs, including telephone lines to the university for information and referral, on-site support groups, and a respite program with the company sharing the costs.[10,11]

The American Association of Retired Persons has also become involved. A project called Caregivers in the Workplace is designed to learn about the problems faced by employees. The survey given to employees at five companies is crafted to learn about the responsibilities that employees have for relatives. Based on the response, ten training modules will be developed for employees to better understand the issues.[12]

With fewer hospitalizations and shorter lengths of stay, elderly patients are returning to the community more quickly. This frequently occurs without the benefits of an effective discharge plan and when they are more acutely ill. This often leaves elderly patients and their families grappling with a long-term care system that is inadequate, fragmented, and expensive.

Corporate America's entry into exploring the problems of an elderly care system is a positive sign. With an increased awareness of the problems of employees, corporations can turn their talents and energy to addressing the financing and delivery of a long-term care system for the elderly.

NOTES

1. N. R. Kleinfield, "When the Boss Becomes Your Doctor," *New York Times,* January 5, 1986, p. 25.

2. Ibid.

3. Joseph Califano, Jr., "A Corporate Rx for America: Managing Runaway Health Costs," *Issues in Science and Technology,* Spring 1986, pp. 87–88.

4. David Streitfield, "Balancing Work and Eldercare," *Washington Post,* July 29, 1986, sec. C, p. 5.

5. Dana E. Friedman, "Eldercare: The Employee Benefit of the 1990's," *Across the Board,* June 1986, pp. 45–46.

6. Barbara Greenberg, Administrator, Older Americans Initiative. Telephone conversation on December 9, 1986.

7. Friedman, "Eldercare," pp. 46–47.

8. Ibid., p. 47.

9. Michael Creedom, Principal Investigator, Administration on Aging Grant to University of Bridgeport Center for the Study of Aging. Phone conversation on December 16, 1986.

10. Friedman, "Eldercare," p. 47.

11. Creedom, phone conversation on December 16, 1986.

12. Friedman, "Eldercare," p. 48.

Chapter 13

Summary

Patricia A. O'Hare
Margaret A. Terry

13

Discharge planning, or continuity of care planning, is of paramount importance for the survival of many health care organizations and for the provision of quality patient care. The process of individually assessing, planning, and implementing care plans with patients to ensure continuing appropriate care is the approach. Developing this approach into a well-organized, efficient system is the challenge to professionals and organizations.

Discharge planning has been operationalized in this book. The discharge planning process has been explored. Information has been shared on how to design, implement, and evaluate discharge planning programs. The need for linkages has been identified. These linkages must now become functional throughout all components of the health care delivery system. We have emphasized the skills and knowledge needed by those professionals involved in the process. The complexity and difficulty of arranging feasible plans in a health care system that has not supported this activity and frequently does not have the resources to attain needed goals have been examined. Discharge planning has entered a new era. It is no longer the responsibility of only a few professionals who recognize its importance. Health care administrators now are recognizing the benefits and the necessity of these programs. The incentives are beginning to be placed within the health care system to develop discharge planning programs for ongoing care. This book reviews the economic, legal, and competitive incentives that are encouraging health care organizations to set up discharge planning programs. The organizations in which the incentives are strongest (i.e., hospitals and health maintenance organizations) are moving more quickly into developing programs and approaches.

However, there are major issues that cast a shadow on this provision of care and establishment of linkages within the health care system. Approximately 35 million persons in the United States are without health insurance,[1] and that number continues to grow. "Between 1980 and 1982 the proportion of the nation's poor without either Medicaid or private health insurance coverage rose by 20 percent, while the amount of free care provided by the country's hospitals increased by less than 4 percent."[2] As presented at a congressional hearing, "nearly half of the medically uninsured are full-time workers and their dependents and one-third are part-time workers."[3] Policy approaches to address the problem might include hospital assistance programs and employer requirements through federal legislation for the provision of health insurance benefits to their employees and their dependents. As another option Senator Donald Riegle (D-Mich.), a member of the Senate Finance Committee, has introduced S. 177, the Health Care for the Uninsured Act, that would mandate the establishment of state health care risk pools for hard-to-insure people, with premiums based on a sliding scale.[4] This critical issue left unresolved will result in fewer choices, less access, more fragmentation of services, and even total lack of care.

The lack of an affordable, coordinated long-term care system bankrupts the aged and the disabled and stagnates their movement through the system. There is limited private long-term care insurance available, and Medicare was not designed to pay for long-term care. "Most nursing home care is financed by private family resources, and 40 percent is paid by Medicaid, the nation's fiscally strapped insurance program for the poor."[5] The out-of-pocket costs in home care services are devastating, both personally and financially. The average cost for one year of 40-hour-per-week homemaker and personal care aide services approaches $20,000.

These issues are unresolved because there are marked differences in the way Americans feel about questions such as the following:

- What are the rights and responsibilities of individuals, government, and the private sector in health care?
- If better health care is a right, what level of care must be provided? Is a two- or three-tier system of care acceptable to Americans?
- Who pays for that care?
- From what revenue sources should publicly financed programs be paid?
- Can an egalitarian-oriented America provide publicly financed second- or third-tier care? Can the federal government avoid such questions by leaving coverage problems in state hands?[6]

In this era of cost containment, movement of patients to less costly levels of care is encouraged and frequently mandated. The time is right for the meshing of the incentives, standards, and mandates. The expertise of nursing and social work always present is being strengthened. With the standards as developed by the professionals and the mandates not only from the Health Care Financing Administration, but also from organizations such as the American Hospital Association, the Joint Commission on Accreditation of Hospitals, the National Association for Home Care, and others, new and stronger programmatic changes will occur. The postdischarge system is inadequately funded. The reimbursement mechanisms need to be changed. The current trends in the direction of coverage for only medically defined care and not for the other crucial social support services need to be corrected. The number of people without access to basic health care must be addressed. There needs to be accountability for patient outcomes throughout the system.

Discharge planning has been established as the interorganizational link in ongoing care. How effectively the discharge planning process is implemented will influence the quality of health care and the health of the public both today and in the future.

NOTES

1. U.S. Bureau of the Census, *Statistical Abstract of the United States:* 1986, 106th ed. (Washington, D.C.: Government Printing Office, 1985), p. 101.

2. Robert J. Blendon, "Health Policy Choices for the 1990's," *Issues in Science and Technology* 2, no. 4 (Summer 1986): 70.

3. Helen Darling, "The Role of the Federal Government in Assuring Access to Health Care," *Inquiry* 23, no. 3 (Fall 1986): 286.

4. Howard Buck, "Washington Report," *Discharge Planning Update* 7, no. 4 (May-June 1987): 18.

5. Blendon, "Health Policy Choices for the 1990's," p. 71.

6. Darling, "The Role of the Federal Government," p. 288.

REFERENCES

Cohodes, D.R. "America: The Home of the Free, the Land of the Uninsured." *Inquiry* 23 (Fall 1986): 227–35.

Curtis, R. "The Role of State Governments in Assuring Access to Care." *Inquiry* 23 (Fall 1986): 277–85.

Etheredge, L. "Ethics and the New Insurance Market." *Inquiry* 23 (Fall 1986): 308–15.

Grossman, J.H. "Community Commitment Competition and the Future of Academic Medical Centers." *Inquiry* 23 (Fall 1986): 245–52.

Merrill, J.C., and Somers, S.A. "The Changing Health Care System: A Challenge for Foundations." *Inquiry* 23 (Fall 1986): 316–21.

Sherlock, D.B. "Indigent Care in Rational Markets." *Inquiry* 23 (Fall 1986): 261–67.

Tilly, J., and Brunner, D. *Medicaid Eligibility and Its Effect on the Elderly.* Washington, D.C.: American Association of Retired Persons, January 1987.

Index

About the Editors

Patricia A. O'Hare, Dr. P.H., M.S., R.N. is Assistant Professor of Nursing at Georgetown University School of Nursing, and a Curriculum Advisory Board member at the National Institute for Discharge Planning and Continuity of Care. She is a consultant in discharge planning/continuity of care, and will soon chair the National Committee to Explore the Issue of Certification for Continuing Care Professionals of the American Association for Continuity of Care. Dr. O'Hare's contributions to professional journals include the guest editorial for *Discharge Planning Update* published by the American Hospital Association Society for hospital social work directors.

Margaret A. Terry, M.S., A.N.P.C., R.N. is on the faculty of the Gradduate Program in Home Health Administration at the School of Nursing, Catholic University of America. She also taught management skills for nurses in primary care in the Executive Programs of the Harvard School of Public Health. She's a consultant to home health agencies, hospitals and geriatric facilities, and the Associate Director for Community and Home Health Services at the Greater Southeast Community Hospital in Washington, D.C., where she developed a hospital-wide discharge planning program involving multiple disciplines. Ms. Terry planned, organized, and managed a hospital-based home health agency and freestanding home health agency. She's a board member and now secretary of Capital Home Health Association in Washington, D.C.